SITU

CHINESE

Medical Treatment

醫療華語300句

策劃　梁欣榮
LEUNG, YAN WING
主編　陳立元
CHEN, LI YUAN
作者　柴菁菁
CHAI, JING JING

國家圖書館出版品預行編目資料

> 醫療華語300句／柴菁菁 著－－
> 一版，－臺北市：書林，2010 [民99]
> 面；公分 －
> ISBN 978-957-445-394-8 （平裝附 MP3 光碟片）
> 1. 漢語 2. 讀本
>
> 802.86   99020977

Published by Bookman Books, Ltd.
3F, 60, Roosevelt Rd. Sec. 4, Taipei 100, Taiwan

Situational Chinese: Medical Treatment
醫療華語300句

作　　　　者	柴菁菁	
譯　　　　者	薄瑞安	
執 行 編 輯	劉怡君　吳宛津	
英 文 校 對	Lynn Sauvé	
封 面 設 計	徐子婷	
校　　　　對	柴菁菁　林靜慧　王建文	
出 版 者	書林出版有限公司	
地　　　　址	100 台北市羅斯福路四段60號三樓	
電　　　　話	02-23684938・02-23687226	
傳　　　　真	02-23688929・02-23636630	
發 行 人	蘇正隆	
出 版 經 理	蘇恆隆	
台北書林書店	106 台北市新生南路三段88號2樓之5	Tel: 02-2365-8617
北 區 業 務 部	106 台北市羅斯福路四段60號3樓	Tel: 02-2368-7226
中 區 業 務 部	403 台中市五權路2之143號6樓	Tel: 04-2376-3799
南 區 業 務 部	802 高雄市五福一路77號2樓之1	Tel: 07-229-0300
郵 政 劃 撥	15743873書林出版有限公司	
網　　　　址	http://www.bookman.com.tw	
經 銷 代 理	紅螞蟻圖書有限公司	
	台北市內湖區舊宗路2段121巷28號4樓	
	電話02-2795-3656(代表號)　傳真02-2795-4100	
登 記 證	局版臺業字第一八三一號	
出 版 日 期	2010年12月一版	
定　　　　價	NT$ 250　US$10.00	
I S B N	978-957-445-394-8	

欲利用本書全部或部份內容者，須徵得書林出版有限公司同意或書面授權。

*本書顧及中英詞語對照及英文的表達流暢，部分英文錄音與文字略有出入。

SITUATIONAL CHINESE

Medical Treatment
醫療華語300句

Foreword

The aim of the *Situational Chinese* series is to offer a homogenous set of vocabulary and usage for a targeted rhetorical situation. Aside from an emphasis on a coherent communicative context where Chinese is put to focused but agile use, the series stands out in a market where there already exist similar products in that all its volumes are edited based on a sound pedagogy that eases the progressive challenge of linguistic items for maximum acquisition. Senior ICLP teachers and Chinese experts met regularly, in long sessions, to calibrate each vocabulary item and structure to draw a roadmap for effective Chinese learning. These efforts and expertise are purposely made transparent in the final product so that the volumes will not become ponderous texts that please only the Chinese scholar or serious linguist. What the reader sees is a non-menacing guide with a user-friendly format and plenty of samples that can be put to immediate use.

I came up with the idea of a handy guide series for Chinese learners some years ago when I edited ESL materials for a consumer market that was literally saturated with thousands of books. But while the EFL or ESL pedagogy is already mature enough to authorize all sorts of publications, the Chinese as a second or foreign language concept has yet to grow into a solid branch of knowledge with a comprehensive research basis. As such I needed as much help as I could get from experts in second or foreign language acquisition as well as from teachers on the front line who have documented enough problems in the Chinese classroom to offer practical advice. The empirical approach proved invaluable. Years of teaching has produced insights and prognoses that rival the analyses of statisticians. I want to thank all ICLP teachers and individuals who have contributed time and expertise to the *Situational Chinese* series to make learning standard Chinese a fraction easier, even for those who are about to do it for the first time.

Yanwing Leung, Director
The International Chinese Language Program
National Taiwan University

總序

　　情境華語系列編輯宗旨為提供特定溝通情境內所需的詞彙和慣用語。除了強調如何在相關溝通背景下靈活運用華語，此系列更以精準的教學法編寫，深入淺出的解說，幫助讀者獲得極大的華語學習成效。ICLP的資深教師群和華語專家為了制定這套有效學習華語的方法，花費心力開會討論和校對書中的一字一句。於成書中所刻意淡化的學術專業鑿痕，是因為這套書不是為了討好華語學者或語言學家而出版，而是要以讀者、使用者為主，提供大量能讓讀者立即上手使用的例句。

　　幾年前我在編撰英語學習教材時，那時的消費市場早已充斥著無數英語學習的出版品，我想到為華語學習者編出一套隨手可用的指引手冊。現在EFL或ESL的教學理論愈趨成熟，讓相關的出版品能蓬勃發展。但華語做為第二語言或外語學習的概念尚待茁壯成長，成為一門以全面綜合研究為基礎的學問。因而站在第一線的教師提供給我的幫助不亞於第二語言學家或外語學家的觀點。這些老師們詳細了解華語課堂上會發生的狀況，更能提供實用的建議。這些實證方法是無價的。長年教學經驗而生的洞見與方針也不是統計學家的分析數值可比擬的。

　　我由衷感謝ICLP全體教師和為出版這套華語學習書籍貢獻心力的所有人，也因為他們的付出和專業讓學習華語輕鬆了幾分，即使是初學者也能輕易入門。

梁欣榮

Preface

Medical Treatment

Many people bring along medicine when traveling abroad. One reason is the comfort of familiar brand names and legible instructions. Another is to avoid seeing a doctor abroad. Isn't this just common sense? But unless you are prepared to bring a small pharmacy with you in your suitcase, this strategy won't work on long trips.

A trip to the doctor's isn't anyone's idea of a good time. One reason is the difficulty encountered in communicating with medical professionals. Many ailments are difficult to describe in your own language, let alone in a foreign tongue. Furthermore, when in another country, you may find yourself unfamiliar with the local health care system. In a foreign culture you will likely encounter attitudes toward health, sickness and treatment quite different from your own. For these reasons, many people avoid medical care when abroad except in emergencies.

Perhaps you are new to the Chinese language and are afraid of not being able to communicate at all. Or, perhaps you've already mastered everyday conversation, but are still unfamiliar with the expressions needed at the doctor's office. Perhaps your Chinese is quite strong, but you have yet to acquire specialized medical vocabulary. No matter what your current level of Chinese is, this practical little book will prove an indispensable companion for life in Chinese-speaking places. It provides concise phrases and sentences that you will find immediately useful. It is organized into sections which correspond to different medical fields which makes it useful in any common medical situation.I have also included cultural notes where East and West customs differ substainally.

In Chinese, we often say that a minor illness left untreated will surely become a major one. When this is the case, neither your state of mind nor your wallet is the better for it. I wish you all good health, but if you should fall ill in the Chinese-speaking world, why not take out this little book and muster the courage to speak up and help yourself!

序言

醫療篇

　　很多人不喜歡去看醫生，不知道該怎麼說就是其中的原因之一，如果不是明顯可見的外傷，那些體內的疼痛，即使使用母語似乎也很難正確的描述，何況是外國語呢？再加上外國人對當地的醫療制度和設施都不熟悉，因此除非大病，要不然很少去看醫生。

　　很多人出國的時候，總是隨身帶著藥物，一來是因為對藥物的效用有把握，二來又省了去看醫生的麻煩。是啊！所有的旅遊書不都是這麼建議的嗎？但是短期旅行還可以，忍個幾天就回國了；要是得住個一年半載呢？難道也要拖到回國嗎？難道要把可能用到的藥品都帶夠份量嗎？可能有人真是如此，但這終究不是辦法。

　　外國話說得不好，怕說不清楚，怕聽不懂？有可能。能說一點外國話，但課本中除了簡單的對話以外，並沒有相符的情境能讓我套用？這倒是真的。外國話聽說都沒問題，但是疾病的名稱可能是個障礙？沒錯。這麼看來，就得有一本工具書能消除以上這些憂慮。本書利用簡單的語句，幫助初學者立即可用。按照醫院的科別分類，滿足各種需要。常見疾病和身體各部位的索引，讓你自由運用。

　　中國人說小病不治拖成大病，勞神又傷財。所以有病就去看醫生吧！希望所有的讀者都健康；但若是在華人世界遭遇病痛，不妨拿起這本書，勇敢的開口吧！

Contents

An Introduction to the Chinese Language

Shou-hsin Teng, PhD
Professor of Chinese Linguistics

China is a multi-ethnic society, and when people in general study Chinese, 'Chinese' usually refers to the Beijing variety of the language as spoken by the Han people in China, also known as Mandarin Chinese or simply Mandarin. It is the official language of China, known mostly domestically as Putonghua, the lingua franca, or Hanyu, the Han language. In Taiwan, Guoyu refers to the national/official language, and Huayu to either Mandarin Chinese as spoken by Chinese descendants residing overseas, or to Mandarin when taught to non-Chinese learners (cf. the title of this book). The following pages present an outline of the features and properties of Chinese. For further details, readers are advised to consult various and rich on-line resources.

Language Kinship

Languages in the world are grouped together on the basis of language affiliation, called language-family. Chinese, or rather Hanyu, is a member of the Sino-Tibetan family, which covers most of China today, plus parts of Southeast Asia. Therefore, Tibetan, Burmese, and Thai are genetically related to Hanyu.

Hanyu is spoken in about 75% of the present Chinese territory, by about 75% of the total Chinese population, and it covers 7 major dialects, including the better known Cantonese, Hokkienese, Hakka and Shanghainese.

Historically, Chinese has interacted highly actively with neighboring but unaffiliated languages, such as Japanese, Korean and Vietnamese. The interactions took place in such areas as vocabulary items, phonological structures, a few grammatical features and most importantly the writing script.

Typological Features of Chinese

Languages in the world are also grouped together on the basis of language characteristics, called language typology. Chinese has the following typological traits, which highlight the dissimilarities between Chinese and English.

A. Chinese is a non-tense language. Tense is a grammatical device such that the verb changes according to the time of the event in relation to the time of utterance. Thus 'He talks nonsense' refers to his habit, while 'He talked nonsense' refers to a time in the past when he behaved that way, but he does not necessarily do that all the time. 'Talked' then is a verb in the past tense. Chinese does not operate with this device but marks the time of events with time expressions such as 'today' or 'tomorrow' in the sentence. The verb remains the same regardless of time of happening. This type of language is labeled as an atensal language, while English and most European languages are tensal languages. Knowing this particular trait can help European learners of Chinese avoid mistakes to do with verbs in Chinese. Thus, in responding to 'What did you do in China last year?' Chinese is 'I teach English (last year)'; and to 'What are you doing now in Japan?' Chinese is again 'I teach English (now)'.

B. Nouns in Chinese are not directly countable. Nouns in English are either countable, e.g. 2 apples, or non-countable, e.g. some salt, while all nouns in Chinese are non-countable. When they are to be counted, a measure, or called classifier, must be used between a noun and a number, e.g. 2-piece-candy. Thus, Chinese is a classifier language. Only non-countable nouns in English are used with measures, e.g. a drop of water.

Therefore it is imperative to learn nouns in Chinese together with their associated measures/classifiers. There are only about 30 high-frequency measures/classifiers in Chinese to be mastered at the initial stage of learning.

C. Chinese is a Topic-Prominent language. Sentences in Chinese quite often begin with somebody or something that is being talked about, rather than the subject of the verb in the sentence. This item is called a topic in linguistics. Most Asian languages employ topic, while most European languages employ subject. The following bad English sentences, sequenced below per frequency of usage, illustrate the topic structures in Chinese.

*Senator Kennedy, people in Europe also respected.

*Seafood, Taiwanese people love lobsters best.

*President Obama a, he attended Harvard University.

Because of this feature, Chinese people tend to speak 'broken' English, whereas English speakers tend to sound 'complete', if bland and alien, when they talk in Chinese. Through practice and through keen observations of what motivates the use of a topic in Chinese, this feature of Chinese can be acquired eventually.

D. Chinese tends to drop things in the sentence. The 'broken' tendencies mentioned above also include not using nouns in a sentence where English counterparts are 'complete'. This tendency is called dropping, as illustrated below through bad English sentences.

Are you coming tomorrow? -----   *Come!

What did you buy? -----   *Buy some jeans.

*This bicycle, who rides? -----   *My old professor rides.

The first example drops everything except the verb, the second drops the subject, and the third drops the object. Dropping happens when what is dropped is easily recoverable or identifiable from the contexts or circumstances. Not doing this, Europeans often receive comments that their sentences in Chinese are too often inundated with unwanted pronouns!!

Phonological Characteristics of Chinese

Phonology refers to the system of sound, the pronunciation, of a language. To untrained ears, Chinese language sounds unfamiliar, sort of alien in a way. This is due to the fact that the Chinese sound system contains some elements that are not part of the sound systems of European languages, though commonly found on the Asian continent. These features will be explained below.

On the whole, the Chinese sound system is not really very complicated. It has 7 vowels, 5 of which are found in English (i, e, a, o, u), plus 2 which are not (-e,); and it has 21 consonants, 15 of which are quite common, plus 6 which are less common (zh, ch, sh, r, z, c). And Chinese has a fairly simple syllable shape, i.e. CV plus possible nasals (n or ng). What is most striking to English speakers is that every syllable in Chinese has a 'tone', as will be detailed directly below. But, a word on the sound representation, the pinyin system, first.

A. Hanyu Pinyin. Hanyu Pinyin is a variety of Romanization systems that attempt to represent the sound of Chinese through the use of Roman letters (abc…). Since the end of the 19th century, there have been about half a dozen Chinese Romanization systems, including the Wade-Giles, Guoyu Luomazi, Yale, Hanyu Pinyin, Lin Yutang, and Zhuyin Fuhao Di'ershi, not to mention the German system, the French system etc. Thanks to the consensus of media worldwide, and through the support of the UN, Hanyu Pinyin has become the standard worldwide. Taiwan is probably the only place in the world that does not support nor employ Hanyu Pinyin. Instead, it uses non-Roman symbols to represent the sound, called Zhuyin Fuhao, alias BoPoMoFo (cf. the symbols employed in this volume). Officially, that is. Hanyu Pinyin represents the Chinese sound as follows.

b, p, m, f	d, t, n, l	g, k, h	j, q, x	zh, ch, sh, r	z, c, s
a, o, -e, e	ai, ei, ao, ou		an, en, ang, eng		-r, i, u, ü

B. Chinese is a tonal language. A tone refers to the voice pitch contour. Pitch contours are used in many languages, including English, but for different functions in different languages. English uses them to indicate the speaker's viewpoint, e.g. 'well' in different contours may indicate impatience, surprise, doubt etc. Chinese, on the other hand, uses contours to refer to different meanings, words. Pitch contours with different linguistic functions are not transferable from one language to another. Therefore, it would be futile trying to learn Chinese tones by looking for or identifying their contour counterparts in English.

Mandarin Chinese has 4 distinct tones, the fewest among all Han dialects, i.e. level, rising, dipping and falling, marked ─ ˊ ˇ ˋ , and it has only one tone-change rule, i.e. ˇ ˇ => ˊ ˇ , though the conditions for this change are fairly complicated. In addition to the four tones, Mandarin also has one neutral(ized) tone, i.e. • , pronounced short/unstressed, which is derived, historically if not synchronically, from the 4 tones; hence the term neutralized. Again, the conditions and environments for the neutralization are highly complex and cannot be explored in this space.

C. Syllable final –r effect (vowel retroflexivisation). The northern variety of Hanyu, esp. in Beijing, is known for its richness—the –r effect at the end of a syllable. For example, 'flower' is 'huā' in southern China but 'huār' in Beijing. Given the prominence of the city Beijing, this sound feature tends to be defined as standard nationwide; but that –r effect is rarely attempted in the south. There do not seem to be rigorous rules governing what can and what cannot take the –r effect. It is thus advised that learners of Chinese resort to rote learning in this case, as probably even native speakers of northern Chinese do.

D. Syllables in Chinese do not 'connect'. 'Connect' here refers to the merging of the tail of a syllable with the head of a subsequent syllable, e.g. English pronounces 'at' + 'all' as 'at+tall', 'did' +'you' as 'did+dyou' and 'that'+'is' as 'that+th'is'. On the other hand, syllables in Chinese are isolated from each other and do not connect in this way. Fortunately, this is not a serious problem for English language learners, as the syllable structures in Chinese are rather limited, and there are not many candidates for this merging. We noted above that Chinese syllables take the form of CV plus possible 'n' and 'ng'. CV does not give rise to connecting, not even in English; so be extra cautious when a syllable ends with 'n' or 'g' and a subsequent syllable begins with a V, e.g. MǐnÀo 'Fujian Province and Macao'. Nobody would understand 'min+nao'!!

E. Retroflexive consonants. 'Retroflexive' refers to consonants that are pronounced with the tip of the tongue curled up (-flexive) backwards (retro-). There are altogether 4 such consonants, i.e. zh, ch, sh, and r. The pronunciation of these consonants reveals the geographical origin of native Chinese speakers. Southerners do not have them, merging them with z, c, and s, as is commonly observed in Taiwan. Curling up of the tongue comes in various degrees. Local Beijing dialect is well known for its prominent curling. Imagine curling up the tongue at the beginning of a syllable and curling it up again for the –r effect!! Try 'zhèr-over here', 'chóngr-worm' and 'shuǐr-water'.

On Chinese Grammar

'Grammar' refers to the ways and rules of how words are organized into a string that is a sentence in a language. Given the fact that all languages have sentences, and at the same time non-sentences, all languages including Chinese have grammar. In this section, the most salient and important features and issues of Chinese grammar will be presented, but a summary of basic structures, as referenced against English, is given first.

A. Similarities in Chinese and English.

	English	Chinese
SVO	They sell coffee.	Tāmen mài kāfēi.
AuxV+Verb	You may sit down!	Nǐ kěyǐ zuòxià!
Adj+Noun	sour grapes	suān pútao
Prep+its Noun	at home	zài jiā
Num+Meas+Noun	a piece of cake	yíkuài dàngāo
Demons+Noun	those students	nàxiē xuésheng

B. Dissimilar structures.

	English	Chinese
RelClause: Noun	the book that you bought	nǐ mǎide shū
VPhrse: PrepPhrse	to eat at home	zài jiā chī fàn
Verb: Adverbial	Eat slowly!	Mànmār chī!
Set: Subset	6th Sept, 1967	1967 nián 9 yuè 6 hào
	Taipei, Taiwan	Táiwān Táiběi
	? of my friends...	Wǒde pengyou, yǒu sānge.

C. Modifier precedes modified (MPM). This is one of the most important grammatical principles in Chinese. We see it operating actively in the charts given above, so that adjectives come before the nouns they modify, relative clauses also come before the nouns they modify, possessives come before nouns (tāde diànnǎo 'his computer'), auxiliary verbs come before verbs, adverbial phrases before verbs, prepositional phrases come before verbs etc. This principle operates almost without exception in Chinese, while in English modifiers sometimes precede and sometimes follow the modified.

D. Principle of Temporal Sequence (PTS). Components of a sentence in Chinese are lined up in accordance with the sequence of time. This principle operates especially when there is a series of verbs contained within a sentence, or when there is a sentential conjunction. First compare the sequence of 'units' of an event in English and that in its Chinese counterpart.

Event: David /went to New York/ by train /from Boston/ to see his sister.

English: 1   2   3   4   5
Chinese: 1   4   3   2   5

Now in real life, David got on a train, the train departed from Boston, it arrived in New York, and finally he visited his sister. This sequence of units is 'natural' time, and the Chinese sentence 'Dàwèi cóng Bōshìdùn zuò huǒchē dào Niǔyuē qù kàn tāde jiějie' follows it, but not English. In other words, Chinese complies strictly with PTS.

When sentences are conjoined, English has various possibilities in organizing the conjunction. First, the scenario. H1N1 hits China badly (event-1), and as a result, many schools were closed (event-2). Now, English has the following possible ways of conjoining to express this, e.g.

Many schools were closed, because/since H1N1 hit China badly. (E2+E1)

H1N1 hit China badly, so many schools were closed. (E1+E2)

As H1N1 hit China badly, many schools were closed. (E1+E2)

Whereas the only way of expressing the same in Chinese is E1+E2 when both conjunctions are used (yīnwèi…suǒyǐ…), i.e.

Zhōngguó yīnwèi H1N1 gǎnrǎn yánzhòng (E1), suǒyǐ xǔduō xuéxiào zhànshí guānbì (E2).

PTS then helps explain why 'cause' is always placed before 'consequence' in Chinese.

PTS is also seen operating in the so-called verb-complement constructions in Chinese, e. shā-sǐ 'kill+dead', chī-bǎo 'eat+full', dǎ-kū 'hit+cry' etc. The verb represents an action that must have happened first before its consequence.

There is an interesting group of adjectives in Chinese, namely 'zǎo-early', 'wǎn-late', 'kuài-fast', 'màn-slow', 'duō-plenty', and 'shǎo-few', which can be placed either before (as adverbials) or after (as complements) of their associated verbs, e.g.

Nǐ míngtiān zǎo diǎr lái! (Come earlier tomorrow!)

Wǒ lái zǎo le. Jìnbuqù. (I arrived too early. I could not get in.)

When 'zǎo' is placed before the verb 'lái', the time of arrival is intended, planned, but when it is placed after, the time of arrival is not pre-planned, maybe accidental. The difference complies with PTS. The same difference holds in the case of the other adjectives in the group, e.g.

Qǐng nǐ duō mǎi liǎngge! (Please get two extra!)

Wǒ mǎiduō le. Zāota le! (I bought two too many. Going to be wasted!)

'Duō' in the first sentence is going to be pre-planned, a pre-event state, while in the second, it's a post-event report. Pre-event and post-event states then are naturally taken care of by PTS. Our last set in the group is more complicated. 'Kuài' and 'màn' can refer to amount of time in addition to manner of action, as illustrated below.

Nǐ kuài diǎr zǒu; yào chídào le! (Hurry up and go! You'll be late (e.g. for work)!

Qǐng nǐ zǒu kuài yīdiǎr! (Please walk faster!)

'Kuài' in the first can be glossed as 'quick, hurry up' (in as little time as possible after the utterance), while that in the second refers to manner of walking. Similarly, 'màn yīdiǎr zǒu-don't leave yet' and 'zǒu màn yīdiǎr-walk more slowly'.

We have seen in this section the very important role in Chinese grammar played by variations in word-order. European languages exhibit rich resources in changing the forms of verbs, adjectives and nouns, and Chinese, like other Asian languages, takes great advantage of word-order.

E. Where to find subjects in existential sentences. Existential sentences refer to sentences in which the verbs express appearing (e.g. coming), disappearing (e.g. going) and presence (e.g. written (on the wall)). The existential verbs are all intransitive, and thus they are all associated with a subject, without any objects naturally. This type of sentence deserves a mention in this introduction, as they exhibit a unique structure in Chinese. When their subjects are in definite reference (something that can be referred to, e.g. pronouns and nouns with definite article in English), the subject appears at the front of the sentence, i.e. before the existential verb, but when their subjects are in indefinite reference (nothing in particular), the subject appears after the verb. Compare the following pair of sentences in Chinese against their counterparts in English.

Kèrén dōu lái le. Chī fàn ba! (All the guests we invited have arrived. Let's serve the dinner.)

Duìbùqǐ! Láiwǎn le. Jiāli láile yíge kèrén. (Sorry for being late! I had an (unexpected) guest.)

More examples of post-verbal subjects are given below.

Zhècì táifōng sǐle bùshǎo rén. (Quite a few people died during the typhoon this time.)

Zuótiān wǎnshang xiàle duō jiǔ de yǔ? (How long did it rain last night?)

Zuótiān wǎnshang pǎole jǐge fànrén? (How many inmates got away last night?)

Chēzili zuòle duōshǎo rén a? (How many people were in the car?)

Exactly when to place the existential subject after the verb will remain a challenge for learners of Chinese for quite a significant period of time. You have to observe and deduce.

The existential subjects presented above are simple enough, e.g. people, a guest, rain and inmates. But when the subject is complex, further complications emerge!! A portion of the complex subject stays in front of the verb, and the remaining goes to the back of the verb, e.g.

Míngtiān nǐmen qù jǐge rén? (How many of you will be going tomorrow?)

Wǒ zuìjìn diàole bùshǎo tóufǎ. (I lost=fell quite a lot of hair recently.)

Qùnián dìzhèn, tā sǐle sānge gēge. (He lost=died 3 brothers during the earthquake last year.)

In linguistics, we say that existential sentences in Chinese have a lot of semantic and information structures involved.

F. A tripartite system of verb classifications in Chinese. English has a clear division between verbs and adjectives, but the boundary in Chinese is quite blurred, which quite seriously misleads English-speaking learners of Chinese. The error in *Wǒ jīntiān shì máng. 'I am busy today.' is a daily observation in Chinese 101! Why is it a common mistake for beginning learners? What do our textbooks and/or teachers do about it, so that the error is discouraged, if not suppressed? Nothing, much! What has not been realized in our profession is that Chinese verb classification is more strongly semantic, rather than more strongly syntactic as in English.

Verbs in Chinese have 3 sub-classes, namely Action Verbs, State Verbs and Process Verbs. Action Verbs are time-sensitive activities (beginning and ending, frozen with a snap-shot, prolonged), are will-controlled (consent or refuse), and usually take human subjects, e.g. 'chī-eat', 'mǎi-buy' and 'xué-learn'. State Verbs are non-time-sensitive physical or mental states, inclusive of the all-famous adjectives as a further sub-class, e.g. 'ài-love', 'xīwàng-hope' and 'liàng-bright'. Process Verbs refer to instantaneous change from one state to another, 'sǐ-die', 'pò-break, burst' and 'wán-finish'.

The new system of parts of speech in Chinese as adopted in this series is built on the very foundation of this tripartite verb classification. Knowing this new system will be immensely helpful in learning quite a few syntactic structures in Chinese that are nicely related to the 3 classes of verbs, as will be illustrated with negation in Chinese in the section below.

The table below presents some of the most important properties of these 3 classes of verbs, as reflected through syntactic behaviour.

	Action Verbs	State Verbs	Process Verbs
Hěn- modification	✗	✓	✗
Le- completive	✓	✗	✓
Zài- progressive	✓	✗	✗
Reduplication	✓ (tentative)	✓ (intensification)	✗
Bù- negation	✓	✓	✗
Méi- negation	✓	✗	✓

Here are more examples of 3 classes of verbs.

Action Verbs: mǎi 'buy', zuò 'sit', xué 'learn; imitate', kàn 'look'.

State Verbs: xǐhuān 'like', zhīdào 'know', néng 'can', guì 'expensive'.

Process Verbs: wàngle 'forget', chén 'sink', bìyè 'graduate', xǐng 'wake up'.

G. Negation. Negation in Chinese is by means of placing a negative adverb immediately in front of a verb. (Remember that adjectives in Chinese are a type of State verb!) When an action verb is negated with 'bu', the meaning can be either 'intend not to, refuse to' or 'not in a habit of', e.g.

Nǐ bu mǎi piào; wǒ jiù bú ràng nǐ jìnqu! (If you don't buy a ticket, I won't let you in!)

Tā zuótiān zhěng tiān bù jiē diànhuà. (He did not want to answer the phone all day yesterday.)

Dèng lǎoshī bù hē jiǔ. (Mr. Teng does not drink.)

'Bù' has the meaning above but is independent of temporal reference. The first sentence above refers to the present moment or a minute later after the utterance, and the second to the past. A habit again is panchronic. But when an action verb is negated with 'méi(yǒu)', its time reference must be in the past, meaning 'something did not come to pass', e.g.

Tā méi lái shàngbān. (He did not come to work.)

Tā méi dài qián lái. (He did not bring any money.)

A state verb can only be negated with 'bù', referring to the non-existence of that state, whether in the past, at present, or in the future, e.g.

Tā bù zhīdào zhèjiàn shì. (He did not/does not know this.)

Tā xiǎng gēn nǐ qù. (He wants/wanted to go with you.)

Niǔyuē zuìjìn bú rè. (New York was/is/will not be hot.)

A process verb can only be negated with 'méi', referring to the non-happening of a change from one state to another, usually in the past, e.g.

Yīfu méi pò; nǐ jiù rēng le? (You threw away perfectly good clothes?)

Niǎo hái méi sǐ; nǐ jiù fàng le ba! (The bird is still alive. Why don't you set it free?)

Tā méi bìyè yǐqián, hái děi dǎgōng. (He has to work odd jobs before graduating.)

As can be gathered from the above, negation of verbs in Chinese follows neat patterns, but this is so only after we work with the new system of verb classifications as presented in this series. Here's one more interesting fact about negation in Chinese before closing this section. When some action verbs refer to some activities that result in something stable, e.g. when you put on clothes, you want the clothes to stay on you, the negation of those verbs can be usually translated in the present tense in English, e.g.

Tā zěme méi chuān yīfuu?? (How come he is naked?)

Wǒ jīntiān méi dài qián. (I have no money with me today.)

H. A new system of Parts of Speech in Chinese. In the system of parts of speech adopted in this series, there are at the highest level a total of 8 parts of speech, as given below. This system includes the following major properties. First and foremost, it is errors-driven and can address some of the most prevailing errors exhibited by learners of Chinese. This characteristic dictates the depth of sub-categories in a system of grammatical categories. Secondly, it employs the concept of 'default'. This property greatly simplifies the over-all framework of the new system, so that it reduces the number of categories used, simplifies the labeling of categories, and takes advantage of the learners' contribution in terms of positive transfer. And lastly, it incorporates both semantic as well as syntactic concepts, so that it bypasses the traditionally problematic category of adjectives by establishing three major semantic types of verbs, viz. action, state and process.

Adv	Adverb (dōu 'all', dàgài 'probably')
Conj	Conjunction (gēn 'and', kěshì 'but')
Det	Determiner (zhè 'this', nà 'that')
M	Measure (ge, tiáo; xià, cì)
N	Noun (wǒ 'I', yǒngqì 'courage')
Part	Particle (ma 'question particle', le 'completive verbal particle')
Prep	Preposition (cóng 'from', duìyú 'regarding')
V	Action Verb, transitive (mǎi 'buy', chī 'eat')
Vi	Action Verb, intransitive (kū 'cry', zuò 'sit')
Vaux	Auxiliary Verb (néng 'can', xiǎng 'would like to')
V-sep	Separable Verb (jiéhūn 'get married', shēngqì 'get angry')
Vs	State Verb, intransitive (hǎo 'good', guì 'expensive')
Vst	State Verb, transitive (xǐhuān 'like', zhīdào 'know')
Vs-attr	State Verb, attributive (zhǔyào 'primary', xiùzhēn 'mini-')
Vs-pred	State Verb, predicative (gòu 'enough', duō 'plenty')
Vp	Process Verb, intransitive (sǐ 'die', wán 'finish')
Vpt	Process Verb, transitive (pò (dòng) 'lit. break (hole) , liè (fèng) 'lit. crack (a crack))

Notes:

Default values: When no marking appears under a category, a default reading takes place, which has been built into the system by observing the commonest patterns of the highest frequency. A default value can be loosely understood as the most likely candidate. A default system results in using fewer symbols, which makes it easy on the eyes, reducing the amount of processing. Our default readings are as follows.

Default transitivity. When a verb is not marked, i.e. V, it's an action verb. An unmarked action verb, furthermore, is transitive. A state verb is marked as Vs, but if it's not further marked, it's intransitive. The same holds for process verbs, i.e. Vp is by default intransitive.

Default position of adjectives. Typical adjectives occur as predicates, e.g. 'This is *great*!' Therefore, unmarked Vs are predicative, and adjectives that cannot be predicates will be marked for this feature, e.g. zhǔyào 'primary' is an adjective but it cannot be a predicate, i.e. *Zhètiáolù hěn zhǔyào. '*This road is very primary.' Therefore it is marked Vs-attr, meaning it can only be used attributively, i.e. zhǔyào dàolù 'primary road'. On the other hand, 'gòu' 'enough' in Chinese can only be used predicatively, not attributively, e.g. 'Shíjiān gòu' '*Time is enough.', but not *gòu shíjiān 'enough time'. Therefore gòu is marked Vs-pred. Employing this new system of parts of speech guarantees good grammar!

Default wordhood. In English, words cannot be torn apart and be used separately, e.g. *mis- not –understand. Likewise in Chinese, e.g. *xǐbùhuān 'do not like'. However, there is a large group of words in Chinese that are exceptions to this probably universal rule and can be separated. They are called 'separable words', marked -sep in our new system of parts of speech. For example, shēngqì 'angry' is a word, but it is fine to say *shēng* tā *qì* 'angry at him'. Jiéhūn 'get married' is a word but it's fine to say *jiéguòhūn* 'been married before' or *jiéguò* sāncì *hūn* 'been married 3 times before'. There are at least a couple of hundred separable words in modern Chinese. Even native speakers have to learn that certain words can be separated. Thus, memorizing them is the only way for learners to deal with them, and our new system of parts of speech helps them along nicely. Go over the vocabulary lists in this series and look for the marking –sep.

Now, what motivates this severing of words? Ask Chinese gods, not your teachers! We only know a little about the syntactic circumstances under which they get separated. First and foremost, separable words are in most cases intransitive verbs, whether action, state or process. When these verbs are further associated with targets (nouns, conceptual objects), frequency (number of times), duration (for how long), occurrence (done, done away with) etc., separation takes pace and these associated elements are inserted in between. More examples are given below.

Wǒ jīnnián yǐjīng *kǎo*guò 20cì *shì* le!! (I've taken 20 exams to date this year!)

Wǒ *dào*guò *qiàn* le; tā hái shēngqì! (I apologized, but he's still mad!)

Fàng sāntiān *jià*; dàjiā dōu zǒu le. (There will be a break of 3 days, and everyone has left.)

Final Words

This is a very brief introduction to the modern Mandarin Chinese language, which is the standard world-wide. This introduction can only highlight the most salient properties of the language. Many other features of the language have been left out by design. For instance, nothing has been said about the patterns of word-formations in Chinese, and no presentation has been made of the unique written script of the language. Readers are advised to search on-line for resources relating to particular aspects of the language. For reading, please consult a highly readable best-seller in this regard, viz. Li, Charles and Sandra Thompson. 1981. *Mandarin Chinese: a reference grammar*. University of California Press.

Shou-hsin Teng, PhD
Professor of Chinese Linguistics
University of Massachusetts, Amherst, Mass, USA (retired)
National Taiwan Normal University, Taipei, Taiwan (retired)
Maa Fa Luang University, Chiang Rai, Thailand (current)
November 2009

SITUATIONAL CHINESE

Medical Treatment

Medical Treatment
醫療篇

Unit One: You've Discovered You're Sick
單元一：發現症狀

Unit Two: Seeking Aid　單元二：詢求協助

Unit Three: General Questions　單元三：一般詢問

Unit Ten: Doctors' Directions　單元十：醫生的指示

Unit One: You've Discovered You're Sick
單元一：發現症狀

General Symptoms ▌ 一般症狀

001 我 身體 不 太 舒服。
Wǒ shēntǐ bu tài shūfu.
我 身体 不 太 舒服。
I don't feel very well.

002 我 好像 生病 了。
Wó hǎoxiàng shēngbìng le.
我 好像 生病 了。
I may be coming down with something.

003 我 想 我 感冒 了。
Wó xiáng wó gǎnmào le.
我 想 我 感冒 了。
I think I have a cold.

Cold Symptoms ▌ 感冒症狀

004 我 的 頭 很 暈。
Wǒ de tóu hěn yūn.
我 的 头 很 晕。
I feel dizzy/lightheaded.

005 我 想 吐。
Wó xiǎng tù.
我 想 吐。
I feel like I'm going to throw up.

006 我 有 一點兒 發燒。
Wó yǒu yìdiǎr fāshāo.
我 有 一点儿 发烧。
I have a mild fever.

Keyword				
暈	yūn	晕	to be dizzy	Vs
吐	tù	吐	to throw up	V
發燒	fāshāo	发烧	have a fever	Vp

Ear, Nose, and Throat Symptoms
耳、鼻、喉症狀

007 我 喉嚨 痛。
Wǒ hóulóng tòng.
我 喉咙 痛。
I have a sore throat.

008 我 的 耳朵 有 一點兒 不對勁.
Wǒ de ěrduo yǒu yìdiǎr búduìjìn.
我 的 耳朵 有 一点儿 不对劲。
There's something wrong with my ears.

009 我 流 鼻血 了。
Wǒ liú bíxiě le.
我 流 鼻血 了。
My nose is bleeding.

Keyword				
喉嚨	hóulóng	喉咙	throat	N
痛	tòng	痛	to be sore	Vs
不對勁	búduìjìn	不对劲	something wrong	Vs
流鼻血	liú bíxiě	流鼻血	nose is bleeding	◎

◎: not a part of speech in Chinese.

Gastrointestinal Symptoms and Allergies
▌腸胃和過敏症狀

010 我 從 昨晚 開始，就 覺得 胃 不 太 舒服。
Wǒ cóng zuówǎn kāishǐ, jiù juéde wèi bú tài shūfu.
我 从 昨晚 开始，就 觉得 胃 不 太 舒服。
My stomach has been upset since last night.

011 我 肚子 好 痛。
Wǒ dùzi hǎo tòng.
我 肚子 好 痛。
My stomach hurts a lot.

012 不 知道 什麼 東西 讓 我 過敏 了。
Bù zhīdao shénme dōngxi ràng wǒ guòmǐn le.
不 知道 什么 东西 让 我 过敏 了。
I'm having an allergic reaction to something.

Keyword				
胃	wèi	胃	stomach	N
過敏	guòmǐn	过敏	allergic	Vi

Stings and Animal Bites ▌ 叮、咬

013 我 被 蜜蜂 螫 了 一下。
Wǒ bèi mìfēng zhē le yíxia.
我 被 蜜蜂 螫 了 一下。
I was stung by a bee.

014 我 快 被 蚊子 咬死 了。
Wǒ kuài bèi wénzi yáosǐ le.
我 快 被 蚊子 咬死 了。
I'm being eaten alive by mosquitos.

015 那 隻 狗 咬 了 我 的 腳踝。
Nà zhī gǒu yǎo le wǒ de jiǎohuái.
那 只 狗 咬 了 我 的 脚踝。
That dog bit me on the ankle.

Keyword				
蜜蜂	mìfēng	蜜蜂	bee	N
螫	zhē	螫	to sting	V
蚊子	wénzi	蚊子	mosquito	N
腳踝	jiǎohuái	脚踝	ankle	N

Skin Wounds ▍ 皮膚外傷

016 我 被 熱水 燙傷 了。
Wǒ bèi rèshuǐ tàngshāng le.
我 被 热水 烫伤 了。
I scalded myself with hot water.

017 我 的 肩膀 曬傷 了。
Wǒ de jiānbǎng shàishāng le.
我 的 肩膀 晒伤 了
My shoulders got sunburned.

018 我 的 腳後跟 破皮 了。
Wǒ de jiǎohòugēn pòpí le.
我 的 脚后跟 破皮 了。
The skin on my heel got rubbed off.

Keyword				
燙傷	tàngshāng	烫伤	to scald	V
肩膀	jiānbǎng	肩膀	shoulder(s)	N
曬傷	shàishāng	晒伤	to be sunburn	V
腳後跟	jiǎohòugēn	脚后跟	heel	N
破皮	pòpí	破皮	skin is rubbed off	V-sep

Sprains and Muscle Aches ▌扭傷、痠痛

019 我 的 腳 **扭傷** 了。
Wǒ de jiǎo niǔshāng le.
我 的 脚 扭伤 了。
I twisted my ankle.

020 我 的 **膝蓋** **撞到** 桌子，瘀青 了。
Wǒ de xīgài zhuàngdào zhuōzi, yūqīng le.
我 的 膝盖 撞到 桌子，瘀青 了。
I banged my knee on the table and bruised it.

021 我 腰酸 背痛*。
Wǒ yāosuān bèitòng.
我 腰酸 背痛。
I have a sore back.

* 「腰酸背痛 yāosuān bèitòng」: Chinese differentiates between the lower
back (腰 yāo) and upper back (背 bèi)。「腰酸背痛」includes both words
and functions as a predicate meaning that one's entire back is in pain.
「腰酸背痛」may be caused by anything from a slipped disk to poor
posture. Since severe back pain may radiate into the chest，「腰酸背痛」
may refer generally to soreness throughout the upper body.

Keyword				
扭傷	niǔshāng	扭伤	to injure by twisting	Vi
膝蓋	xīgài	膝盖	knee	N
撞到	zhuàngdào	撞到	to strike with force	V
瘀青	yūqīng	瘀青	bruise	N

Unit Two: Seeking Aid
單元二：詢求協助

Seeking General Assistance
▌請求一般性的協助

022 你 可 不 可 以 送 我 去 醫院？
Nǐ ké bu kéyǐ sòng wǒ qù yīyuàn?
你 可 不 可 以 送 我 去 医院？
Could you take me to the hospital?

023 你 可 不 可 以 幫 我 叫 救護車？
Nǐ ké bu kéyǐ bāng wǒ jiào jiùhùchē?
你 可 不 可 以 帮 我 叫 救护车？
Could you help me call an ambulance?

024 你 可 不 可 以 幫 我 聯絡 我 的 家人？
Nǐ ké bu kéyǐ bāng wǒ liánluò wǒ de jiārén?
你 可 不 可 以 帮 我 联络 我 的 家人？
Would you inform my family, please?

Keyword				
救護車	jiùhùchē	救护车	ambulance	N
聯絡	liánluò	联络	to inform	V

請 你 扶 我 站 起來。

Qíng nǐ fú wǒ zhàn qǐlai.

请 你 扶 我 站 起来。

Please help me stand up.

 請 你 幫 我 打 電話 掛號*。

Qíng nǐ bāng wó dǎ diànhuà guàhàn

请 你 帮 我 打 电话 挂号。

Please help me call and make an appointment.

* 「掛號 guàhào」: Taiwanese hospitals and clinics generally employ a system of registration by number called 「掛號」 to determine the order in which patients are seen. Thus rather than making an appointment for a specifc time, you come during the doctor's hours and wait your turn. You may register in advance by telephone or in person to speed things up.

 請 你 幫 我 填 這 張 初診單**。

Qíng nǐ bāng wǒ tián zhè zhāng chūzhěndān.

请 你 帮 我 填 这 张 初诊单。

Please help me fill out this medical history form.

** 「初診單 chūzhěndān」: On the first visit to a hospital or clinic, one usually completes a 「初診單」 "first appointment form" (the the chart on the reverse side). It may also be called a 「初診病歷表 chūzhěn bìnglìbiǎo」.

Keyword				
初診單	chūzhěndān	初诊单	medical history form	N

Calling for Help in Emergencies ▌ 緊急求救

 **救命！**
Jiùmìng!
救命！
Help!

029 快 打 電話 給一一九。
Kuài dǎ diànhuà gěi yīyījiǔ.
快 打 电话 给一一九。
Call 119 right away.

030 這裡 需要 救護車。
Zhèlǐ xūyào jiùhùchē.
这里 需要 救护车。
I need an ambulance.

Keyword				
救命	jiùmìng	救命	help	V-sep

031 這裡 有 人 昏倒 了。
Zhèlǐ yǒu rén hūndǎo le.
这里 有 人 昏倒 了。
Someone fainted.

032 這裡 有 人 噎著 了。
Zhèlǐ yǒu rén yēzháo le.
这里 有 人 噎著 了。
Someone is choking.

033 這裡 有 人 受 重傷 了。
Zhèlǐ yǒu rén shòu zhòngshāng le.
这里 有 人 受 重伤 了。
Someone is seriously injured.

Keyword				
昏倒	hūndǎo	昏倒	to faint and fall down	Vp
噎著	yēzháo	噎著	to choke on something	V
受重傷	shòu zhòngshāng	受重伤	to suffer a serious injury	◎

Unit Three: General Questions
單元三：一般詢問

Asking about Doctors ▎ 詢問醫生

034 你 知道 哪 一 個 醫生 看得 比較 好？
Nǐ zhīdao nǎ yí ge yīshēng kànde bǐjiào hǎo?
你 知道 哪 一 个 大夫* 看得 比较 好？
Do you know which doctor is better?
* In Mainland China, a doctor is called 大夫 (dàifu).

035 你 有 沒有 給 這 個 醫生 看過 病？
Ní yǒu méiyǒu gěi zhèi ge yīshēng kànguò bìng?
你 有 没有 给 这 个 大夫 看过 病？
Have you ever been to this doctor?

036 這裡 的 醫生 會 不會 說 英文？
Zhèlǐ de yīshēng huì buhuì shuō Yīngwén?
这里 的 大夫 会 不会 说 英文？
Do the doctors here speak English?

Asking about Hospitals ▎ 詢問醫院

 請問，王 醫生 的 看診 時間 是 什麼 時候？
Qǐngwèn, Wáng yīshēng de kànzhěn shíjiān shì shénme shíhou?

请问，王 大夫 的 看诊 时间 是 什么 时候？
Excuse me, what are Dr. Wang's hours for seeing patients?

 我 得 現場 掛號* 還是 可以 預約 掛號**？
Wó děi xiànchǎng guàhào háishì kéyǐ yùyuē guàhào?

我 得 现场 挂号 还是 可以 预约 挂号？
Do I make an appointment once I get there or can I do it ahead of time?

* 「現場掛號 xiànchǎng guàhào」: You may go to a hospital or clinic during the doctor's hours, register, and then wait your turn. This is the most common procedure.

** 「預約掛號 yùyuē guàhào」: To reduce waiting time you can preregister via phone, internet, or in person. Registration personnel will give you an estimate of the time this number will be called. If you are late, notify the hospital and they will reinsert your number later in the sequence.

 這裡 看診 最 晚 到 什麼 時候？
Zhèlǐ kànzhěn zuì wǎn dào shénme shíhou?

这里 看诊 最 晚 到 什么 时候？
What time do you stop seeing patients?

Keyword				
看診	kànzhěn	看诊	to see a patient	Vi
現場	xiànchǎng	现场	on site	N
預約	yùyuē	预约	to make an appointment	V

Asking about the Location of Hospitals and Clinics ▌ 詢問醫療地點

040 最近 的 **藥局** 在 哪裡？
Zuìjìn de yàojú zài nálǐ?
最近 的 药局 在 哪里？
Where's the nearest pharmacy?

041 這 附近 有 **牙科 診所** 嗎？
Zhè fùjìn yǒu yákē zhénsuǒ ma?
这 附近 有 牙科 诊所 吗？
Is there a dental clinic nearby?

042 台大 醫院 離 這兒 多 遠？
Táidà Yīyuàn lí zhèr duó yuǎn?
台大 医院 离 这儿 多 远？
How far is National Taiwan University Hospital from here?

Keyword				
藥局	yàojú	药局	pharmacy	N
牙科	yákē	牙科	the dental department	N
診所	zhěnsuǒ	诊所	clinic	N

Asking about Fees ▋ 詢問費用

043 我 保 了 旅遊險。
Wó bǎo le lǚyóuxiǎn.
我 保 了 旅游险。
I have travel insurance.

044 如果 保險 不 給付，我 得 付 多 少 錢？
Rúguǒ báoxiǎn bù jǐfù, wó děi fù duō shao qián?
如果 保险 不 给付，我 得 付 多 少 钱？
How much will this cost if my insurance won't cover it?

045 我 能 不 能 用 信用卡 付款？
Wǒ néng bunéng yòng xìnyòngkǎ fùkuǎn?
我 能 不 能 用 信用卡 付款？
Do you accept credit cards?

Keyword				
旅遊險	lǚyóuxiǎn	旅游险	travel insurance	N
保險	bǎoxiǎn	保险	insurance	N
給付	jǐfù	给付	to pay	V
付款	fùkuǎn	付款	to pay	V-sep

這 張 收據 包括 了 所有 的 項目 嗎？
Zhè zhāng shōujù bāokuò le suóyǒu de xiàngmù ma?

这 张 收据 包括 了 所有 的 项目 吗？
Does this invoice include everything?

 這裡 只 收 現金 嗎？
Zhèlǐ zhǐ shōu xiànjīn ma?

这里 只 收 现金 吗？
Do you only take cash?

 你 可 不 可以 先 告訴 我 要 付 多少 錢？
Nǐ ké bu kéyǐ xiān gàosu wǒ yào fù duō shao qián?

你 可 不 可以 先 告诉 我 要 付 多 少 钱？
Can you tell me how much it's going to cost ahead of time?

Keyword

收據	shōujù	收据	invoice	N
所有	suóyǒu	所有	all	Vs-attr
項目	xiàngmù	项目	item	N

Looking for Things at the Drugstore
▍在藥房詢問藥品位置

049
對不起，請問 OK繃 放 在 哪裡？
Duìbuqǐ, qǐngwèn, OK bēng fàng zài nálǐ?
对不起， 请问 OK绷 放 在 哪里？
Excuse me, where can I find Band-Aids?

050
請問，**眼藥水** 在 哪 一 **排**？
Qǐngwèn, yǎnyàoshuǐ zài nǎ yì pái?
请问， 眼药水 在 哪 一 排？
Which aisle are eyedrops in?

051
你 能 不 能 幫 我 找 這 個 藥？
Nǐ néng bunéng bāng wó zhǎo zhèi ge yào?
你 能 不 能 帮 我 找 这 个 药？
Could you please help me find this medicine?

Keyword				
OK繃	OK bēng	OK绷	Band-Aids	N
眼藥水	yǎnyàoshuǐ	眼药水	eyedrops	N
排	pái	排	a row	M

Asking about Medicine at the Drugstore
❚ 在藥房詢問有關藥品的問題

 你們 有 沒有 什麼 藥 可以 **治 鼻塞**？
Nǐmen yǒu méiyǒu shénme yào kéyǐ zhì bísāi?
你们 有 没有 什么 药 可以 治 鼻塞？
Do you have anything for a stuffy nose?

 哪 一 種 **止痛藥** 比較 好？
Nǎ yì zhǒng zhǐtòngyào bǐjiào hǎo?
哪 一 种 止痛药 比较 好？
What's the best kind of pain-killer?

 嘴 破 了，要 **擦** 哪 種 **藥膏**？
Zuǐ pò le, yào cā ná zhǒng yàogāo?
嘴 破 了，要 擦 哪 种 药膏？
What should I put on a split lip?

Keyword				
治	zhì	治	to control	V
鼻塞	bísāi	鼻塞	to have a stuffy nose	Vi
止痛藥	zhǐtòngyào	止痛药	pain-killer	N
擦	cā	擦	to apply (liquid or ointment)	V
藥膏	yàogāo	药膏	ointment	N

Unit Four: Medical Questions
單元四：醫療專業詢問

Asking about Your Condition ▌ 詢問自己的病情

055 我 的 病 很 嚴重 嗎？
Wǒ de bìng hěn yánzhòng ma?
我 的 病 很 严重 吗？
Do you think it's serious?

056 我 需要 住院 嗎？
Wǒ xūyào zhùyuàn ma?
我 需要 住院 吗？
Do I need to be hospitalized?

057 這 個 病 要 多 久 才 會 好？
Zhèi ge bìng yào duó jiǔ cái huì hǎo?
这 个 病 要 多 久 才 会 好？
How long will it take to get better?

Keyword				
嚴重	yánzhòng	严重	serious	Vs

058 我 的 病 要 開刀 嗎？
Wǒ de bìng yào kāidāo ma?
我 的 病 要 开刀 吗？
Will I need surgery?

059 什麼 時候 還要 回診？
Shénme shíhou háiyào huízhěn?
什么 时候 还要 回诊？
When should I come back for another appointment?

060 這 段 期間，吃 東西 要 特別 注意 嗎？
Zhè duàn qíjiān, chī dōngxi yào tèbié zhùyì ma?
这 段 期间，吃 东西 要 特别 注意 吗？
Is there anything I should or shouldn't eat while I am taking the medication?

Keyword				
回診	huízhěn	回诊	to be examined again	Vi
段	duàn	段	a measure word of time	M
期間	qíjiān	期间	time/period	N
注意	zhùyì	注意	to pay attention to	V

061 怎麼樣 可以 好 得 快 一點兒？
Zěnmeyàng kéyǐ hǎo de kuài yìdiǎr?
怎么样 可以 好 得 快 一点儿？
Is there anything I can do to speed up my recovery?

062 還有 其他 治療 方法 嗎？
Hái yǒu qítā zhìliáo fāngfǎ ma?
还 有 其它 治疗 方法 吗？
Is there any other treatment?

063 這個病 好 了 以後，還會 不會 復發？
Zhèi ge bìng hǎo le yǐhòu, hái huì buhuì fùfā?
这 个 病 好 了 以后，还 会 不 会 复发？
After I'm better, is there a risk of it happening again?

Keyword				
其他	qítā	其它	other	Vs-attr
治療	zhìliáo	治疗	to treat	V
方法	fāngfǎ	方法	method	N
復發	fùfā	复发	to relapse	Vp

Asking about Medicines ▌ 詢問用藥情形

064 這 個 藥 會 讓 人 想 睡 覺 嗎 ？
Zhèi ge yào huì ràng rén xiǎng shuìjiào ma?
这 个 药 会 让 人 想 睡 觉 吗？
Will this medicine make me feel sleepy?

065 這 個 藥 怎 麼 吃 ？
Zhèi ge yào zěnme chī?
这 个 药 怎 么 吃？
What's the dosage?

066 這 種 藥 可 以 用 多 久 ？
Zhè zhǒng yào kéyǐ yòng duó jiǔ?
这 种 药 可 以 用 多 久？
How long can I use this medicine?

這 個 藥 有 沒 有 **副作用**？
Zhèi ge yào yǒu méiyǒu fùzuòyòng?
这 个 药 有 没 有 副作用？
Are there any harmful side effects?

 吃 這 個 藥 有 沒 有 什麼 要 注意 的？
Chī zhèi ge yào yǒu méiyǒu shénmo yào zhùyì de?
吃 这 个 药 有 没 有 什么 要 注意 的？
Is there anything to watch out for when taking this medicine?

 這 種 藥 和 我 平 常 吃 的 **降血壓藥** 可以 一起 吃 嗎？
Zhè zhǒng yào hé wǒ píngcháng chī de jiàngxiěyāyào kéyǐ yìqǐ chī ma?
这 种 药 和 我 平 常 吃 的 降血压药 可以 一起 吃 吗？
Can I take this medicine with the blood pressure medication I normally take?

Keyword				
副作用	fùzuòyòng	副作用	side effect	N
降血壓藥	jiàngxiěyāyào	降血压药	blood pressure medication	N

Asking about a Test—Before the Test
詢問檢驗情形—檢驗前

070 做 這 項 檢查 有 危險 嗎？

Zuò zhè xiàng jiǎnchá yǒu wéixiǎn ma?

做 这 项 检查 有 危险 吗？

Is this test dangerous?

071 做 這 項 檢查 會 痛 嗎？

Zuò zhè xiàng jiǎnchá huì tòng ma?

做 这 项 检查 会 痛 吗？

Is this test painful?

072 做 這 項 檢查 要 花 多 少 時間？

Zuò zhè xiàng jiǎnchá yào huā duō shao shíjiān?

做 这 项 检查 要 花 多 少 时间？

How long will this test take?

Keyword				
項	xiàng	项	item	M
檢查	jiǎnchá	检查	test	N
危險	wéixiǎn	危险	to be dangerous	Vs

Asking about a Test—After the Test
▍詢問檢驗情形—檢驗後

073 檢查 結果 怎麼樣？
Jiǎnchá jiéguǒ zěnmeyàng?
檢查 結果 怎么样？
What's the result of the test?

074 檢查 出 病因 是 什麼 了 嗎？
Jiǎnchá chū bìngyīn shì shénme le ma?
檢查 出 病因 是 什么 了 嗎？
What do the test results show?

075 我 為什麼 還要 再 做 進一步 的 檢查？
Wǒ wèishénme háiyào zài zuò jìnyíbù de jiǎnchá?
我 为什么 还要 再 做 进一步 的 檢查？
Why do you have to perform more tests?

Keyword				
結果	jiéguǒ	结果	result	N
病因	bìngyīn	病因	the cause of a disease	N
進一步	jìnyíbù	进一步	further	Adv

Asking about Surgery ▌ 詢問手術的問題

 為什麼 要 動 手術？
Wèishénme yào dòng shǒushù?
为什么 要 动 手术?
Why is surgery necessary?

 不 動 手術 的 話，會 怎麼樣？
Bú dòng shǒushù de huà, huì zěnmeyàng?
不 动 手术 的 话，会 怎么样?
What would happen if I didn't undergo surgery?

078 手術 的 成功率 高 不高？
Shǒushù de chénggōnglǜ gāo bugāo?
手术 的 成功率 高 不高?
How high is the success rate for this surgery?

Keyword				
動手術	dòng shǒushù	动手术	to have surgery	Vi
成功率	chénggōnglǜ	成功率	rate of success	N

Asking about Hospitalization ▎ 詢問住院的問題

079 健保 病房 住 幾 個 人？

Jiànbǎo bìngfáng zhù jǐ ge rén?

健保 病房 住 几 个 人？

How many beds does a standard hospital room hold?

080 我 能 不能 隨時 離開 病房？

Wǒ néng bunéng suíshí líkāi bìngfáng?

我 能 不能 随时 离开 病房？

Am I allowed to leave my room whenever I want?

081 需要 不 需要 有 人 在 病房 照顧 我？

Xūyào bu xūyào yǒu rén zài bìngfáng zhàogù wǒ?

需要 不 需要 有 人 在 病房 照顾 我？

Do I need to have someone in the hospital room to take care of me?

Keyword				
健保	jiànbǎo	健保	health insurance	N
病房	bìngfáng	病房	hospital room	N
照顧	zhàogù	照顾	to take care of	V

082 我 是 不 是 非 吃 醫院 準備 的 **食物** 不可？

Wǒ shì bushì fēi chī yīyuàn zhǔnbèi de shíwù bùkě?

我 是 不 是 非 吃 医院 准备 的 食物 不可？

Do I have to eat food provided by the hospital?

083 如果 我 需要 幫忙 怎麼辦？

Rúguó wǒ xūyào bāngmáng zěnmebàn?

如果 我 需要 帮忙 怎么办？

What should I do if I need assistance?

084 **探病** 時間 是 什麼 時候？

Tànbìng shíjiān shì shénme shíhou?

探病 时间 是 什么 时候？

When are visiting hours?

| 食物 | shíwù | 食物 | food | N |
| 探病 | tànbìng | 探病 | to visit a sick person | V-sep |

Asking about Someone's Condition
▌ 詢問他人病情

085 什麼 時候 可以 知道 結果？
Shíme shíhou kéyǐ zhīdao jiéguǒ?
什么 时候 可以 知道 结果？
When will we know the result?

086 現在 情形 怎麼樣？
Xiànzài qíngxíng zěnmeyàng?
现在 情形 怎么样？
What is his/her condition?

087 他(她) 沒事 吧？
Tā méishì ba?
他(她) 没事吧?
Is he/she okay?

| 沒事 | méishì | 没事 | okay/alright | Id |

Id: an idiom.

Unit Five: Describing Your Symptoms
單元五：症狀描述

Internal Medicine Dept. ▌ 內科

● **Throat** 喉嚨

088 我 喉嚨 痛，連 **吞 口 水** 都 痛。
Wǒ hóulóng tòng, lián tūn kóushuǐ dōu tòng.
我 喉咙 痛，连 吞 口水 都 痛。
My throat hurts. It hurts to swallow.

089 我 喉嚨 有 痰。
Wǒ hóulóng yǒu tán.
我 喉咙 有 痰。
There's mucus in my throat.

090 我 的 喉嚨 **癢癢** 的，但是 咳 不 出 痰 來，就是 **乾咳**。
Wǒ de hóulóng yángyang de, dànshì ké bu chū tán lai, jiùshì gānké.
我 的 喉咙 痒痒 的，但是 咳 不 出 痰 来，就是 干咳。
My throat itches, but I can't cough up any mucus. It's a dry cough.

Keyword

吞口水	tūn kǒushuǐ	吞口水	to swallow saliva	◎
痰	tán	痰	mucus	N
癢	yǎng	痒	to itch	Vs
乾咳	gānké	干咳	dry cough	N

● **Nose** 鼻子

091 我 流 鼻水。
Wǒ liú bíshuǐ.
我 流 鼻水。
I have a runny nose.

092 我 流 鼻涕。
Wǒ liú bítì.
我 流 鼻涕。
I have a lot of mucus in my nose.

093 我 鼻塞 很 嚴重。
Wǒ bísāi hěn yánzhòng.
我 鼻塞 很 严重。
I have a really stuffy nose.

Keyword				
鼻水	bíshuǐ	鼻水	nasal mucus	N
鼻涕	bítì	鼻涕	nasal mucus	N

- **Coughing, sneezing, and wheezing**
  咳嗽、打噴嚏和氣喘

094 我 不 停 地 打 噴 嚏。
Wǒ bù tíng de dǎ pēntì.
我 不 停 地 打 喷 嚏。
I keep sneezing.

095 我 一直 咳嗽，晚上 都 沒 辦法 睡覺。
Wǒ yìzhí késou, wǎnshang dōu méi bànfǎ shuìjiào.
我 一直 咳嗽，晚上 都 没 办法 睡觉。
I can't sleep at night because I keep coughing

096 我 喘 得 很 厲害，快 沒 辦法 呼吸 了。
Wó chuǎn de hěn lìhai, kuài méi bànfǎ hūxī le.
我 喘 得 很 厉害，快 没 办法 呼吸 了。
I'm weezing really badly. I can barely breathe.

Keyword				
打噴嚏	dǎ pēntì	打喷嚏	to sneeze	V-sep
咳嗽	késou	咳嗽	to cough	Vi
喘	chuǎn	喘	to gasp for air	Vi
厲害	lìhài	厉害	badly	Vs
呼吸	hūxī	呼吸	to breathe	Vi

● **Others** 其他

097 我 沒有 聲音 了。
Wǒ méiyǒu shēngyīn le.
我 没有 声音 了。
I've lost my voice.

098 我 全身 沒有 力氣。
Wǒ quánshēn méiyǒu lìqi.
我 全身 没有 力气。
I feel weak all over.

099 我 全身 痠痛。
Wǒ quánshēn suāntòng.
我 全身 酸痛。
I'm sore all over.

Keyword				
力氣	lìqi	力气	strength	N
痠痛	suāntòng	酸痛	to be sore (of a muscle)	Vs

Surgery Dept. ▌外科

100 我 切 菜 的 時候，不 小心 切到 手。
Wǒ qiē cài de shíhou, bù xiǎoxīn qiēdào shǒu.
我 切 菜 的 时候，不 小心 切到 手。
I accidentally cut my finger while I was chopping vegetables.

101 我 被 紙 割傷 了。
Wǒ bèi zhǐ gēshāng le.
我 被 纸 割伤 了。
I got a paper cut.

102 我 受傷 了，流 了 一點兒 血。
Wǒ shòushāng le, liú le yìdiǎr xiě.
我 受伤 了，流 了 一点儿 血。
I got hurt and bled a little bit.

Keyword				
切	qiē	切	to cut	V
割傷	gēshāng	割伤	cut	Vi
流血	liúxiě	流血	to bleed	V-sep

103 我 從 腳踏車 上 摔 下來，膝蓋 擦 破 了 皮。

Wǒ cóng jiǎotàchē shang shuāi xiàlai, xīgài cā pò le pí.

我 从 自行车 上 摔 下来，膝盖 擦 破 了 皮。

I fell off my bike and skinned my knee.

104 我 被 狗 咬 了。

Wǒ bèi gǒu yáo le.

我 被 狗 咬 了。

I was bitten by a dog.

105 我 的 傷口 發炎 了。

Wǒ de shāngkǒu fāyán le.

我 的 伤口 发炎 了。

My wound is infected.

Keyword				
腳踏車	jiǎotàchē	自行车	bicycle	N
摔	shuāi	摔	to fall off	Vi
膝蓋	xīgài	膝盖	knee	N
擦	cā	擦	to rub	V
傷口	shāngkǒu	伤口	wound	N
發炎	fāyán	发炎	to get infected	Vi

Ear, Nose, and Throat Dept. ▎耳鼻喉科

● **Ears** 耳朵

我 常常 **耳鳴**，而且 **聽力 減退**。
Wǒ chángcháng ěrmíng, érqiě tīnglì jiǎntuì.
我 经常 耳鸣，而且 听力 减退。
I often hear a ringing in my ears, and my hearing has gotten worse.

我 的 耳朵 好像 **進水** 了。
Wǒ de ěrduo hǎoxiàng jìnshuǐ le.
我 的 耳朵 好像 进水 了。
There's water in my ears.

好像 有 東西 跑進 我 的 耳朵 裡。
Hǎoxiàng yǒu dōngxi pǎojìn wǒ de ěrduo lǐ.
好像 有 东西 跑进 我 的 耳朵 里。
It seems that there's something in my ear.

Keyword				
耳鳴	ěrmíng	耳鸣	ringing in the ears	N
聽力	tīnglì	听力	hearing	N
減退	jiǎntuì	减退	to get worse	Vp
進水	jìnshuǐ	进水	water gets in	Vi

● **Nose** 鼻子

109 我 常常 流 鼻血。
Wǒ chángcháng liú bíxiě.
我 常常 流 鼻血。
I often get nosebleeds.

110 我 的 鼻子 經常 過敏。
wǒ de bízi jīngcháng guòmǐn.
我 的 鼻子 经常 过敏。
I often suffer from nasal allergies.

111 因為 鼻子 不 通，所以 有 時候 睡覺 會 打呼。
Yīnwèi bízi bù tōng, suóyí yǒu shíhou shuìjiào huì dǎhū.
因为 鼻子 不 通，所以 有 时候 睡觉 会 打呼。
I sometimes snore because my nose is blocked.

Keyword				
鼻子	bízi	鼻子	nose	Adv
經常	jīngcháng	经常	often	N
通	tōng	通	unobstructed	Vi
打呼	dǎhū	打呼	to snore	Vi

● **Throat** 喉嚨

112 我 的 聲音 非常 沙啞。
Wǒ de shēngyīn fēicháng shāyǎ.
我 的 声音 非常 沙哑。
My voice is very hoarse.

113 我 的 **扁桃腺** 好像 **發炎** 了，**吞嚥 困難**。
Wǒ de biǎntáoxiàn hǎoxiàng fāyán le, tūnyàn kùnnán.
我 的 扁桃腺 好像 发炎 了，吞咽 困难。
My tonsils seem to be inflamed. It's hard to swallow.

114 有 **魚刺 卡住** 我 的 喉嚨 了，吞 不 下去，也 咳 不 出來。
Yǒu yúcì kǎzhù wǒ de hóulóng le, tūn bú xiàqu, yě ké bù chūlai.
有 鱼刺 卡住 我 的 喉咙 了，吞 不 下去，也 咳 不 出来。
There's a fishbone stuck in my throat. I can't swallow it or cough it up.

Keyword				
沙啞	shāyǎ	沙哑	to be hoarse	Vs
扁桃腺	biǎntáoxiàn	扁桃腺	tonsil	N
吞嚥困難	tūnyàn kùnnán	吞咽	to be hard to swallow	◎
魚刺	yúcì	鱼刺	fishbone	N
卡住	kǎzhù	卡住	to get stuck in	Vp

Dermatology Dept. ▍皮膚科

● Allergies 過敏

115 我 的 **皮膚** 很 癢。
Wǒ de pífū hén yǎng.
我 的 皮肤 很 痒。
My skin itches.

116 我 好像 過敏 了，全身 起 疹子。
Wó hǎoxiàng guòmǐn le, quánshēn qí zhěnzi.
我 好像 过敏 了，全身 起 疹子。
I seem to be having an allergic reaction. I have a rash all over my body.

117 原來 只是 一些 小 紅點，現在 腫成 一 大 塊。
Yuánlái zhǐshì yìxiē xiǎo hóngdiǎn, xiànzài zhǒngchéng yí dà kuài.
原来 只是 一些 小 红点，现在 肿成 一 大 块。
Before this was just a little red spot, but now it's swollen into a big lump.

Keyword				
皮膚	pífū	皮肤	skin	N
起疹子	qǐ zhěnzi	起疹子	to get of a rash	◎
紅點	hóngdiǎn	红点	red spot	N
腫	zhǒng	肿	to swell	Vs

● **Sunburns, other burns** 曬傷、燙傷

118 我 忘 了 擦 **防曬油**，有 點兒 曬傷。皮膚 又 紅 又 痛。

Wǒ wàng le cā fángshàiyóu, yóu diǎr shàishāng. Pífū yòu hóng yòu tòng.

我 忘 了 擦 防晒油，有 点儿 晒伤。皮肤 又 红 又 痛。

I forgot to use sun block and got a little sunburned. My skin is red and hurts.

119 我 被 熱水 燙傷 了，沖過 冷水 了，可是 大 片 紅腫。

Wǒ bèi rèshuǐ tàngshāng le, chōngguò léngshuǐ le, kěshì dà piàn hóngzhǒng.

我 被 热水 烫伤 了，冲过 冷水 了，可是 大 片 红肿。

I scalded my self with hot water. I ran cold water over the area, but it's red and swollen all over.

120 我 做菜 的 時候，不 小心 燙到 **鍋子**，起了 一 個 **水泡**。

Wǒ zuòcài de shíhou, bù xiǎoxīn tàngdào guōzi, qǐle yí ge shuǐpào.

我 做菜 的 时候，不 小心 烫到 锅子，起了 一 个 水泡。

When I was cooking, I accidentally burned myself on a pot and got a blister.

Keyword

防曬油	fángshàiyóu	防晒油	sunscreen lotion	N
沖	chōng	冲	to pour water	V
鍋子	guōzi	锅子	pot	N
水泡	shuǐpào	水泡	blister	N

● **Peeling, acne, scars** 脫皮、青春痘、疤

121 我 的 皮膚 在 脫皮。
Wǒ de pífū zài tuōpí.
我 的 皮肤 在 脱皮。
My skin is peeling.

122 我 臉上 **長滿** 了 **青春痘**。
Wó liǎnshang zhángmǎn le qīngchūndòu.
我 脸上 长满 了 青春痘。
My face is covered with pimples.

123 我 想 **去掉** 皮膚 上 的 **疤**。
Wó xiǎng qùdiào pífū shang de bā.
我 想 去掉 皮肤 上 的 疤。
I'd like to get rid of this scar.

Keyword				
脫皮	tuōpí	脱皮	to peel	V-sep
長滿	zhǎngmǎn	长满	something grows all over	V
青春痘	qīngchūndòu	青春痘	pimple	N
去掉	qùdiào	去掉	to get rid of	Vp
疤	bā	疤	scar	N

Ophthalmology Dept. ▌ 眼科

 原先 只是 眼睛 很 癢，揉 了 一下，就 腫 起來 了。

Yuánxiān zhǐshì yǎnjīng hén yǎng, róu le yíxia, jiù zhóng qǐlai le.

原先 只是 眼睛 很 痒，揉 了 一下，就 肿 起来 了。

Before my eye was just itchy. After I scratched it, it swelled up.

 最近 我 的 眼睛 很 紅，好像 有 東西 跑 進去 了。

Zuìjìn wǒ de yǎnjīng hěn hóng, hǎoxiàng yǒu dōngxi pǎo jìnqù le.

最近 我 的 眼睛 很 红，好像 有 东西 跑 进去 了。

Lately my eye has been very bloodshot. It seems that something is in it.

Keyword				
原先	yuánxiān	原先	before	Adv
揉	róu	揉	to rub/to knead	V

我 的 眼睛 對 光線 非常 **敏感**，看到 **強光** 就 流 **眼淚**。

Wǒ de yǎnjīng duì guāngxiàn fēicháng míngǎn, kàndào qiángguāng jiù liú yǎnlèi.

我 的 眼睛 对 光线 非常 敏感，看到 强光 就 流 眼泪。

My eyes are very sentitive to light. Bright light makes them watery.

 我 的 **視力** 減退，而且 眼睛 容易 **疲勞**。

Wǒ de shìlì jiǎntuì, érqiě yǎnjīng róngyì píláo.

我 的 视力 减退，而且 眼睛 容易 疲劳。

My eyesight is poor and my eyes tire easily.

Keyword				
敏感	mǐngǎn	敏感	to be sensitive	Vs
強光	qiángguāng	强光	bright light	N
眼淚	yǎnlèi	眼泪	tears	N
視力	shìlì	视力	eyesight	N
疲勞	píláo	疲劳	to be tired	Vs

128 在 光線 不好 的 地方，我 看 不 清楚。

Zài guāngxiàn bù hǎo de dìfang, wǒ kàn bù qīngchǔ.

在 光线 不 好 的 地方，我 看 不 清楚。

I can't see well in poorly lit places.

129 我 感覺 眼前 一直 有 東西 飛來 飛去。

Wó gǎnjué yǎnqián yìzhí yǒu dōngxi fēi lai fēi qu.

我 感觉 眼前 一直 有 东西 飞 来 飞 去。

I see floaters.

Keyword				
感覺	gǎnjué	感觉	to feel	V/N

Physical Therapy Dept. ▌ 復健科

● Lower back, neck 腰、脖子

 我 彎腰 的 時候 很 痛。
Wǒ wānyāo de shíhou hěn tòng.
我 弯腰 的 时候 很 痛。
It hurts to bend over.

 我 閃到 腰* 了。
Wó shǎndào yāo le.
我 闪到 腰 了。
I sprained my lower back.

* 「閃到腰 shǎndàoyāo」 is an injury from pulling the muscles of the lower
back, and causes pain. You cannot use your lower back, and in order to
bend over you must hold on to something for support.

 我 落枕** 了。
Wǒ laòzhěn le.
我 落枕 了。
My neck hurts from not sleeping right.

** 「落枕 làozhěn」 Most people assume that 落枕 is caused by sleeping
in the wrong position and is closely related to the height and position of
one's pillow. People used to sleeping sideways often suffer from
落枕.

Keyword				
彎腰	wānyāo	弯腰	to bend down	Vi
閃到腰	shǎndàoyāo	闪到腰	to sprain your lower back	◎
落枕	luòzhěn	落枕	kneck hurts	Vi

● **Legs, knees** 腳、膝蓋

133 我 在 **樓梯** 上 **踩空** 了，結果 扭傷 了 腳踝。

Wǒ zài lóutī shang cǎikōng le, jiéguó niǔshāng le jiǎohuái.

我 在 楼梯 上 踩空 了，结果 扭伤 了 脚踝。

I missed the last step and twisted my ankle.

134 我 的 膝蓋 很 痛，不 太 能 爬 樓梯 和 **跑步**。

Wǒ de xīgài hěn tòng, bú tài néng pá lóutī hé pǎobù.

我 的 膝盖 很 痛，不 太 能 爬 楼梯 和 跑步。

My knees hurt. I can't really use stairs or run.

135 我 的 腳 感覺 **麻**麻 的，膝蓋 也 不 太 能 彎。

Wǒ de jiáo gǎnjué mámá de, xīgài yě bù tài néng wān.

我 的 脚 感觉 麻麻 的，膝盖 也 不 太 能 弯。

My feet are numb, and I can't really bend my knees.

Keyword				
樓梯	lóutī	楼梯	stairs	N
踩空	cǎikōng	踩空	to step unoccupied	Vi
跑步	pǎobù	跑步	to run	Vi
麻	má	麻	to be numb	Vs

● **Sports injuries** 運動傷害

136 我 好像 脫臼 了，手 只要 一 動 就 會 痛。
Wó hǎoxiàng tuōjiù le, shóu zhǐyào yí dòng jiù huì tòng.
我 好像 脫臼 了，手 只要 一 动 就 会 痛。
It seems I sprained it. My arm hurts whenever I move it a little.

137 我 打 籃球 的 時候，手指 吃 蘿蔔乾* 了。
Wó dǎ lánqiú de shíhou, shóuzhǐ chī luóbógān le.
我 打 篮球 的 时候，手指 吃 萝卜干 了。
I jammed my finger while I was playing basketball.

* 「吃蘿蔔乾 chī luóbógān」Because a swollen finger joint looks like Chinese pickled radish, jamming a finger is called「吃蘿蔔乾」. You may apply a cooling ointment or spray, but don't rub it! That will only exacerbate the damage to your capillaries causing more swelling! Use a glove or bandage to prevent further swelling.

138 我 跑步 的 時候，肌肉 拉傷 了。
Wó pǎobù de shíhou, jīròu lāshāng le.
我 跑步 的 时候，肌肉 拉伤 了。
I pulled a muscle when I was running.

Keyword

脫臼	tuōjiù	脫臼	get dislocated	Vp
只要	zhǐyào	只要	whenever	Conj
手指	shǒuzhǐ	手指	finger	N
肌肉	jīròu	肌肉	muscle	N
拉傷	lāshāng	拉伤	to strain a muscle	Vi

Gastroenterology Dept. ▍腸胃科

● Stomach 胃

139 我 胃 不 舒服。
Wǒ wèi bù shūfu.
我 胃 不 舒服。
I have an upset stomach.

140 我 肚子 脹氣。
Wǒ dùzi zhàngqì.
我 肚子 胀气。
I feel bloated.

141 我 打嗝 打 個 不停。
Wó dǎgé dǎ ge bù tíng.
我 打嗝 打 个 不 停。
I can't seem to stop burping.

Keyword				
脹氣	zhàngqì	胀气	to feel bloated	Vp
打嗝	dǎgé	打嗝	to burp	V-sep

- **Intestine** 腸

142 我 吃 什麼 就 吐 什麼。
Wǒ chī shénme jiù tù shénme.
我 吃 什么 就 吐 什么。
I can't keep anything down.

143 我 一直 拉肚子。
Wǒ yìzhí lā dùzi.
我 一直 拉 肚子。
I keep having diarrhea.

144 我 一直 便秘。
Wǒ yìzhí biànmì.
我 一直 便秘。
I'm constipated.

Keyword				
拉肚子	lā dùzi	拉肚子	to have diarrhea	V-sep
便秘	biànmì	便秘	to be constipated	Vi

The Dentistry Dept. ▋ 牙科

145 我 要 洗牙。
Wǒ yào xǐyá.
我 要 洗牙。
I'd like to have my teeth cleaned.

146 我 的 牙齦 腫 得 很 厲害。
Wǒ de yáyín zhǒng de hěn lìhai.
我 的 牙龈 肿 得 很 厉害。
My gums are very swollen.

147 上排 右邊 第 三 顆 牙 很 痛，痛 得 連 嘴
都 張 不 開 了。
Shàngpái yòubiān dì sān kē yá hěn tòng, tòng de
lián zuǐ dōu zhāng bu kāi le.
上排 右边 第 三 颗 牙 很 痛，痛 得 连 嘴
都 张 不 开 了。
The third tooth to the right on the top hurts so badly that I
can't open my mouth very wide.

Keyword				
洗牙	xǐyá	洗牙	to clean teeth	V-sep
牙齦	yáyín	牙龈	gums	N
顆	kē	颗	measure word for solid, granular or larger things	M
張開	zhāngkāi	张开	to open wide	V

148 我 只要 一 吃 冰 的 東西，**牙齒** 就 很 酸。

Wó zhǐyào yì chī bīng de dōngxi, yáchǐ jiù hěn suān.

我 只要 一 吃 冰 的 东西，牙齿 就 很 酸。

Whenever I eat something cold, my teeth hurt.

149 我 上次 補 的 牙 好像 沒有 補好。

Wǒ shàngcì bǔ de yá hǎoxiàng méiyǒu búhǎo.

我 上次 补 的 牙 好像 没有 补好。

The last filling I got doesn't seem to have been done very well.

150 我 把 門牙 摔斷 了。

Wó bǎ ményá shuāiduàn le.

我 把 门牙 摔断 了。

I broke my front tooth.

Keyword

牙齒	yáchǐ	牙齿	tooth	N
酸	suān	酸	sore	Vs
補牙	bǔyá	补牙	to have a tooth filled	V-sep
門牙	ményá	门牙	front tooth	N
摔斷	shuāiduàn	摔断	to break	V

Chinese Medicine Dept. ▎中醫科

我 一 到 冬天 就 手腳 冰冷，我 想 來 調整 一下 體質*。

Wǒ yí dào dōngtiān jiù shóujiǎo bīnglěng, wó xiǎng lái tiáozhěng yíxia tǐzhí.

我 一 到 冬天 就 手脚 冰冷，我 想 来 调整 一下 体质。

Every winter my feet feel cold. I'd like to modify my overall health.

* 「調整體質 tiáozhěng tǐzhí」: Your 「體質 tǐzhí」, or constitution, determines what illnesses you are particularly susceptible to. For example, those lacking qi 「氣虛 qìxū」 are susceptible to chills. Those with poor digestive systems 「腸胃不好 chángwèi bùhǎo」 often suffer from dyspepsia. Those with a hot constitution 「體熱 tǐrè」 often get fevers. These theories are laid out in ancient Chinese medical treatises. Heredity, environmental factors, age, diet, diseases, and sex life are the six determining factors of 「體質」. 「體質」 is related to bodily fluids, and the vitality of organs, and changes throughout the lifecycle. *The Inner Cannon of Huangdi*《黃帝內經 Huángdì nèijīng》instructs us to 「上工治未病 shàng gōng zhì wèi bìng」—work to treat illnesses which haven't yet manifested. In modern medical terms this could be described as a form of preventative medicine. 「調整體質」 is in essence reaching a higher state of health by diagnosis, and the appropriate modification of diet, exercise and lifestyle. Chinese medicine is also called 「致中和 zhì zhōnghé」的「養生 yǎngshēng」方法。

我 有 **長期** 的 **睡眠** 問題，朋友 介紹 我 來 看 **中醫**。

Wó yǒu chángqí de shuìmián wènti, péngyǒu jièshao wǒ lái kàn Zhōngyī.

我 有 长期 的 睡眠 问题，朋友 介绍 我 来 看 中医。

I have chronic sleep problems. My friend suggested I come here to see a Chinese medicine doctor.

 我 **長期** **使用** 電腦，容易 肩膀 **僵硬**，我 想 推拿* 一下。

Wǒ chángqí shǐyòng diànnǎo, róngyì jiānbǎng jiāngyìng, wó xiǎng tuīná yíxia.

我 长期 使用 计算机，容易 肩膀 僵硬，我 想 推拿 一下。

I use the computer for long periods of time, and my shoulders get stiff easily. I'd like to have a massage.

* 「推拿 tuīná」is a type of massage derived from the Chinese medical and folk treatment traditions. A variety of manual techniques and massage devices are employed to promote health and strengthen the body. Applications range from alleviating pain, to treating orthopoedic conditions--spinal arthritis, slipped disc, arthritis of the shoulder, joint injuries, and dislocations.

Keyword

長期	chángqí	长期	a long period of time	N
睡眠	shuìmián	睡眠	sleep	N
中醫	Zhōngyī	中医	traditional Chinese medicine doctor	N
使用	shǐyòng	使用	to use	V
僵硬	jiāngyìng	僵硬	stiff	Vs

聽說 **針灸***減肥 很 有效，我 想 試試。

Tīngshuō zhēnjiú jiǎnféi hén yóuxiào, wó xiǎng shìshi.

听说 针灸 减肥 很 有效，我 想 试试。

I hear that acupuncture and moxibustion are good for losing weight. I'd like to try it.

*「針灸 zhēnjiǔ」is the collective term for acupuncture and moxibustion, two fields of Chinese medicine. They may be considered forms of physical therapy and are fast, effective, simple, and safe. Separately they are known as「針法」and「灸法」, but are often used in conjuction to treat conditions, and thus are called「針灸」.

In acupuncture, specially made metal needles are inserted into acupoints—particular points on the body. This stimulation harmonizes blood and qi flows, and removes blockages.

In moxibustion, specially prepared mugwort is burned over acupoints. The heat and herbal vapors create a stimulating effect, thus regulating physiological function.

 我 有 **過敏性 鼻炎**，看 醫生 都 看 不 好。

Wó yǒu guòmǐnxìng bíyán, kàn yīshēng dōu kàn bù hǎo.

我 有 过敏性 鼻炎，看 大夫 都 看 不 好。

I have allergy-related rhinitis. Doctors haven't been any help.

Keyword				
針灸	zhēnjiǔ	针灸	acupuncture and moxibustion	N
減肥	jiǎnféi	减肥	to lose weight	V-sep
有效	yǒuxiào	有效	effective	Vs
過敏性 鼻炎	guòmǐnxìng bíyán	过敏性 鼻炎	allergy-related rhinitis	N

我 最近 常常 覺得 **口苦**[*]、口乾，沒有 **胃口**[**]。

Wǒ zuìjìn chángcháng juéde kóukǔ, kǒugān,
méiyǒu wèikǒu.

我 最近 常常 觉得 口苦、口干，没有 胃口。

Lately I've been suffering from bitter mouth, dry mouth,
and a loss of appetite.

[*] 「口苦 kóukǔ」: "bitter mouth" is a common symptom, in which one
feels a bitter taste in the mouth. Drinking water is of no help. In The
Inner Cannon of Huangdi 「口苦」 is listed as a symptom of 「膽痺 dǎnbì」
(parlaysis of the gall bladder). Today it is believed that digestive and
respiratory disorders are the most common cause.

[**] 「胃口 wèikǒu」doesn't just mean the stomach and mouth, but rather
refers to the desire to eat things—appetite. 「沒有胃口 méiyǒu wèikǒu」
means that you don't have an appetite. 「胃口很好 wèikǒu hěnhǎo」
means to have a big appetite.

Keyword				
口苦	kóukǔ	口苦	bitter mouth	Vs
胃口	wèikǒu	胃口	appetite	N

Sleeping Problems ▌ 睡眠障礙

157 我 整晚 翻來 翻去 睡 不 著。
Wǒ zhéngwǎn fān lai fān qu shuì bu zháo.
我 整晚 翻来 翻去 睡 不 著。
I toss and turn all night, and can't get any sleep.

158 我 每天 晚上 大概 只 睡 三 個 鐘頭。
Wó měitiān wǎnshang dàgài zhǐ shuì sān ge zhōngtou.
我 每天 晚上 大概 只 睡 三 个 钟头。
I get about three hours of sleep a night.

159 我 的 鼾聲 很 大。
Wǒ de hānshēng hěn dà.
我 的 鼾声 很 大。
I snore loudly.

Keyword				
整晚	zhěngwǎn	整晚	the whole night	N
翻來翻去	fān lái fān qù	翻来翻去	to turn over and over	Id
睡著	shuìzháo	睡著	to fall asleep	Vp
鼾聲	hānshēng	鼾声	the sound of snoring	N

160 我 總是 睡過頭。
Wǒ zǒngshì shuìguòtóu.
我 总是 睡过头。
I always oversleep.

161 我 每天 晚上 都 會 醒來 好 幾 次。
Wǒ měitiān wǎnshang dōu huì xǐnglái hǎo jǐ cì.
我 每天 晚上 都 会 醒来 好 几 次。
I wake up many times a night.

162 我 最近 老 做 惡夢。
Wǒ zuìjìn lǎo zuò èmèng.
我 最近 老 做 恶梦。
I have been having nightmares lately.

Keyword				
睡過頭	shuìguòtóu	睡过头	to oversleep	Id
醒	xǐng	醒	to wake up	Vp
老	lǎo	老	always	Adv
做惡夢	zuò èmèng	做恶梦	to have a nightmare	◎

Orthopedics Dept. ▌ 骨科

163 我 的 腳踝 是 斷 了，還是 只是 扭傷？
Wǒ de jiǎohuái shì duàn le, háishì zhǐshì niǔshāng?
我的 腳踝 是 斷 了，还是 只是 扭伤？
Is my ankle broken, or is it just a sprain?

164 我 需要 打 石膏 嗎？
Wǒ xūyào dǎ shígāo ma?
我 需要 打 石膏 吗？
Will I need a cast?

165 石膏 要 打 多 久？
Shígāo yào dǎ duó jiǔ?
石膏 要 打 多 久？
How long will I be in a cast?

Keyword				
打石膏	dǎ shígāo	打石膏	to put on a cast	◎

Unit Six: Comforting And Instructing The Sick And Injured
單元六：安慰及指示性的話語

Comforting the Sick and Injured ▎ 安慰病患

166 救護車 已經 在 路上 了。
Jiùhùchē yǐjīng zài lùshang le.
救护车 已经 在 路上 了。
The ambulance is on its way.

167 不要 擔心，不會 有 事 的。
Búyào dānxīn, búhuì yǒu shì de.
不要 担心，不会 有 事 的。
Don't worry. Everything is going to be just fine.

168 我 知道 很 痛，我們 會 送 你 到 醫院 的。
Wǒ zhīdao hěn tòng, wǒmen huì sòng nǐ dào yīyuàn de.
我 知道 很 痛，我们 会 送 你 到 医院 的。
I know it hurts, but we'll get you to the hospital.

Keyword				
擔心	dānxīn	担心	to worry	Vs-sep

Reassuring Those Visiting You in the Hospital
▎ 安慰探病者

169 我 覺 得 好 多 了。
Wǒ juéde hǎo duō le.
我 觉 得 好 多 了。
I feel much better.

170 醫 生 說 我 沒 問 題 了。
Yīshēng shuō wǒ méi wèntí le.
医 生 说 我 没 问 题 了。
The doctor says that I'm fine.

171 我 再 休 息 兩 天 就 可 以 **出 院** 了。
Wǒ zài xiūxi liǎng tiān jiù kéyǐ chūyuàn le.
我 再 休 息 两 天 就 可 以 出 院 了。
I can leave the hospital after resting for two more days.

Keyword				
出院	chūyuàn	出院	to leave the hospital	Vi

Instructing the Sick and Injured ▌ 指示病患

172 儘量 不要 動。
Jǐnliàng búyào dòng.
尽量 不要 动。
Try not to move.

173 不要 睡著，看著 我。
Búyào shuìzháo, kànzhe wǒ.
不要 睡著，看著 我。
Don't fall asleep. Look at me.

174 試著 坐 起來。
Shìzhe zuò qǐlai.
试著 坐 起来。
Try to sit up.

Keyword				
儘量	jǐnliàng	尽量	as best one can	Adv
試著	shìzhe	试著	to try to	Adv

175 試著 走走看。
Shìzhe zóuzoukan.
试著 走走看。
Try to walk.

176 不要 說話，保留 一點兒 體力。
Búyào shuōhuà, bǎoliú yìdiǎr tǐlì.
不要 说话，保留 一点儿 体力。
Don't talk. Save your strength.

177 放輕鬆，深呼吸 幾 下。
Fàngqīngsōng, shēnhūxī jǐ xia.
放轻松，深呼吸 几 下。
Relax. Take a few deep breaths.

Keyword

保留	bǎoliú	保留	to reserve	V
體力	tǐlì	体力	physical strength	N
放輕鬆	fàngqīngsōng	放轻松	to relax	Id
呼吸	hūxī	呼吸	to breathe	V

Unit Seven: Things That The Doctor Might Ask During An Appointment
單元七：醫生看診時的詢問

General Questions ▎ 綜合性詢問

170 哪裡 不 舒服？
Nálǐ bù shūfu?
哪里 不 舒服？
Where does it hurt?

179 哪裡 痛？
Nálǐ tòng?
哪里 痛？
Where's the pain located?

180 身體 有 什麼 問題？
Shēntǐ yǒu shénme wèntí?
身体 有 什么 问题？
What's wrong?

181

還 有 沒有 其他 症狀？

Hái yǒu méiyǒu qítā zhèngzhuàng?

还 有 没有 其它 症状？

Do you have any other symptoms?

182

身體 其他 地方 有 沒有 不 舒服？

Shēntǐ qítā dìfang yǒu méiyǒu bù shūfu?

身体 其它 地方 有 没有 不 舒服？

Are you feeling any discomfort in other areas of your body?

183

家裡 的 人 有 沒有 這 **方面** 的 病？

Jiālǐ de rén yǒu méiyǒu zhè fāngmian de bìng?

家里 的 人 有 没有 这 方面 的 病？

Is there anyone in your family with this kind of disease?

Keyword				
方面	fāngmian	方面	aspect	N

Questions about Cold Symptoms
▌ 詢問感冒症狀

184 發燒 了 嗎？
Fāshāo le ma?
发烧 了 吗？
Do you have a fever?

185 流 鼻水 還是 流 鼻涕？
Liú bíshuǐ háishì liú bítì?
流 鼻水 还是 流 鼻涕？
Is your nose muscus thick or thin?

186 鼻塞 嗎？
Bísāi ma?
鼻塞 吗？
Do you have a stuffy nose?

187 咳嗽 不 咳嗽？

Késou bu késou?

咳嗽 不 咳嗽？

Do you have a cough?/Are you coughing?

188 咳嗽 的 時候 有 沒有 痰？

Késou de shíhou yǒu méiyǒu tán?

咳嗽 的 时候 有 没有 痰？

Are you coughing up any phlegm?

189 吞 東西 的 時候 痛 不痛？

Tūn dōngxi de shíhou tòng butòng?

吞 东西 的 时候 痛 不痛？

Does it hurt to swallow?

Questions about the Duration of Symptoms
詢問症狀期

190 什麼 時候 開始 覺得 不 舒服？
Shénme shíhou kāishǐ juéde bù shūfu?
什么 时候 开始 觉得 不 舒服？
How long have you been feeling this way?

191 你 這 個 **毛病*** 多 久 了？
Nǐ zhèi ge máobìng duó jiǔ le?
你 这 个 毛病 多 久 了？
How long have you been having this problem?

* 「毛病 máobìng」 refers to a variety of minor physical, psychological and behavioral abnomalities, and doesn't correspond perfectly to any one English word. Frequent headaches, a prolonged cough, mood swings, and the proclivity to lose ones keys could all be described as「毛病」.

192 以前 有 沒有 **發生**過 這 種 情形？
Yǐqián yǒu méiyǒu fāshēngguò zhè zhǒng qíngxing?
以前 有 没有 发生过 这 种 情形？
Have you had these symptoms before?

Keyword				
毛病	máobing	毛病	problem	N
發生	fāshēng	发生	to happen	V

Questions about Medications
▌ 藥物的詢問

193 你 會 不 會 對 **藥物** 過敏？

Nǐ huì buhuì duì yàowù guòmǐn?

你 会 不 会 对 药物 过敏？

Are you allergic to any medication?

194 你 是 不 是 正在 **服用** 什麼 藥物？

Nǐ shì bushì zhèngzài fúyòng shénme yàowù?

你 是 不 是 正在 服用 什么 药物？

Are you taking any medications?

195 有 **固定** 服用 的 藥物 嗎？

Yǒu gùdìng fúyòng de yàowù ma?

有 固定 服用 的 药物 吗？

Is there a particular medicine that you always take?

Keyword				
藥物	yàowù	药物	medicine(s)/medication(s)	N
服用	fúyòng	服用	to take	V
固定	gùdìng	固定	fixed	Vs

Questions about Gastrointestinal Symptoms
▌ 詢問腸胃病症狀

196 最近 有 沒有 拉 肚子？
Zuìjìn yǒu méiyǒu lā dùzi?
最近 有 沒有 拉 肚子?
Have you had diarrhea lately?

197 你 是 不是 便秘？
Nǐ shì bushì biànmì?
你 是 不是 便秘?
Are you constipated?

198 你 的 **排便 正常** 嗎？
Nǐ de páibiàn zhèngcháng ma?
你 的 排便 正常 嗎?
Are you having regular bowel movements?

Keyword				
排便	páibiàn	排便	to have a bowel movement	N
正常	zhèngcháng	正常	regularly	Adv

199 你 的 尿 是 什麼 顏色？

Nǐ de niào shì shénme yánsè?

你 的 尿 是 什么 颜色？

What color is your urine?

200 吃 什麼 東西 會 讓 你 脹氣？

Chī shénme dōngxi huì ràng nǐ zhàngqì?

吃 什么 东西 会 让 你 胀气？

What kinds of foods make you bloated?

201 你 有 沒有 想 吐 的 感覺？

Ní yǒu méiyǒu xiǎng tù de gǎnjué?

你 有 没有 想 吐 的 感觉？

Do you feel nauseated?

Keyword				
尿	niào	尿	urine	N

Questions about Lifestyle ▍ 詢問生活習慣

 你 抽 不 抽菸？

Nǐ chōu bu chōuyān?

你 抽 不 抽烟？

Do you smoke?

 你 一 天 抽 幾 根 菸？

Nǐ yì tiān chōu jǐ gēn yān?

你 一 天 抽 几 根 烟？

How many cigarettes do you smoke each day?

204 你 吃 的 夠 不 夠？

Nǐ chī de gòu bugòu?

你 吃 的 够 不 够？

Are you eating enough?

Keyword				
抽菸	chōuyān	抽烟	to smoke	V-sep
根	gēn	根	measure word of a cigarette	N

Questions about Someone's Recent Condition
▎ 詢問近況

205 最近 的 壓力 是 不是 很 大？
Zuìjìn de yālì shì bushì hěn dà?
最近 的 压力 是 不是 很 大？
Have you been feeling stressed lately?

206 最近 有 沒有 去 哪裡 旅行？
Zuìjìn yǒu méiyǒu qù nálǐ lǚxíng?
最近 有 没有 去 哪里 旅行？
Have you traveled anywhere recently?

207 最近 有 沒有 受過 傷？
Zuìjìn yǒu méiyǒu shòuguò shāng?
最近 有 没有 受过 伤？
Have you suffered any injuries lately?

Keyword				
壓力	yālì	压力	pressure	N

Questions about Symptoms at Physical Therapy
▌ 詢問復健科相關病症

 是 哪 種 痛？是 **抽痛** 還是 **刺痛**？

Shì ná zhǒng tòng? Shì chōutòng háishì cìtòng?

是 哪 种 痛？是 抽痛 还是 刺痛？

What kind of pain is it? Is it a throbbing pain or a sharp pain?

 是 肌肉 **疼痛** 還是 **關節** 痛？

Shì jīròu téngtòng háishì guānjié tòng?

是 肌肉 疼痛 还是 关节 痛？

Is it a muscle or joint pain?

210 **通常** 是 什麼 時候 痛？

Tōngcháng shì shénme shíhou tòng?

通常 是 什么 时候 痛？

When does it usually hurt?

Keyword				
抽痛	chōutòng	抽痛	throbbing pain	N
刺痛	cìtòng	刺痛	sharp pain	N
疼痛	téngtòng	疼痛	pain	N
關節	guānjié	关节	joint	N
通常	tōngcháng	通常	usually	Adv

211 你 覺得 肌肉 很 緊 嗎？
Nǐ juéde jīròu hén jǐn ma?
你 觉得 肌肉 很 紧 吗？
Do your muscles feel really stiff?

212 你 的 手 可以 動 嗎？
Nǐ de shǒu kéyǐ dòng ma?
你 的 手 可以 动 吗？
Can you move your arm?

213 你 最近 是 不是 **過度** 使用 這 塊 肌肉？
Nǐ zuìjìn shì bushì guòdù shǐyòng zhè kuài jīròu?
你 最近 是 不是 过度 使用 这 块 肌肉？
Have you overworked this muscle lately?

Keyword				
緊	jǐn	紧	tight	Vs
過度	guòdù	过度	overly	Adv

Questions about Sleeping Problems
▌ 詢問睡眠障礙

214 你 作 惡夢 有 多 久 了？
Nǐ zuò èmèng yǒu duó jiǔ le?
你 作 恶梦 有 多 久 了？
How long have you been having nightmares?

215 你 要 多 久 才 睡得著？
Nǐ yào duó jiǔ cái shuìdezháo?
你 要 多 久 才 睡得著？
How long does it take you to fall asleep?

216 你 一般 睡前 做 些 什麼 事？
Nǐ yìbān shuìqián zuò xiē shénme shì?
你 一般 睡前 做 些 什么 事？
What's your bedtime routine?

一般	yìbān	一般	normally	Adv

217 你 早上 起床 覺得 很 累 嗎？
Ní zǎoshang qǐchuáng juéde hěn lèi ma?
你 早上 起床 觉得 很 累 吗？
Do you feel tired in the morning?

218 你 打鼾 嗎？
Ní dǎhān ma?
你 打鼾 吗？
Do you snore?

219 你 半夜 是 不是 常常 醒來？
Nǐ bànyè shì bushì chángchang xǐnglai?
你 半夜 是 不是 常常 醒来？
Do you wake up in the middle of the night?

Keyword				
打鼾	dǎhān	打鼾	to snore	Vi

Questions about Vision and Eye Problems
▌ 詢問眼睛症狀

220 是 眼睛 裡面 痛 嗎？還是 在 眼睛 周圍？

Shì yǎnjīng lǐmian tòng ma? Háishì zài yǎnjīng zhōuwéi?

是 眼睛 里面 痛 吗？还是 在 眼睛 周围？

Is the pain in the eye, or around the eye?

221 眼睛 瞇 起來 的 時候 痛 不痛？

Yǎnjīng mī qǐlai de shíhou tòng butòng?

眼睛 眯 起来 的 时候 痛 不痛？

Does it hurt when you squint?

222 遠 的 地方 看 得 清楚 嗎？

Yuǎn de dìfang kàn de qīngchǔ ma?

远 的 地方 看 得 清楚 吗？

Are you able to see things clearly at a distance?

Keyword				
周圍	zhōuwéi	周围	around	N
瞇	mī	眯	to squint	V

Questions about Dental Issues ▎ 詢問牙齒問題

 你 有 沒有 **定期** 來 洗牙？
Ní yǒu méiyǒu dìngqí lái xǐyá?
你 有 没有 定期 来 洗牙？
Do you get your teeth cleaned regularly?

 你 有 沒有 用 **牙線**？
Ní yǒu méiyǒu yòng yáxiàn?
你 有 没有 用 牙线？
Do you use floss?

 這 顆 **牙套** 是 什麼 時候 裝 的？
Zhè kē yátào shì shénme shíhou zhuāng de?
这 颗 牙套 是 什么 时候 装 的？
When did you get this crown put in?

Keyword				
定期	dìngqí	定期	regularly	Adv
牙線	yáxiàn	牙线	floss	N
牙套	yátào	牙套	crown	N
裝	zhuāng	装	to put in	V

Unit Eight: Answers To General Questions (See Unit Three)
單元八：回答一般問題(針對單元三)

Recommending Doctors ▎介紹醫生

王醫生看病很**仔細**，你可以**掛**他的**門診**。

Wáng yīshēng kànbìng hén zǐxì, ní kéyǐ guà tā de ménzhěn.

王 大夫 看病 很 仔细，你 可以 挂 他 的 门诊。

Dr. Wang examines patients with a lot of attention to detail. You could make an outpatient appointment.

227 聽說 張 醫生 是 **過敏** 方面 的 **專家**。

Tīngshuō Zhāng yīshēng shì guòmǐn fāngmian de zhuānjiā.

听说 张 大夫 是 过敏 方面 的 专家。

I hear that Dr. Zhang is an expert when it comes to allergies.

Keyword				
仔細	zǐxì	仔细	attentive	Vs
掛	guà	挂	to make	V
門診	ménzhěn	门诊	outpatient services	N
過敏	guòmǐn	过敏	allergy	N
專家	zhuānjiā	专家	expert	N

這裡 的 醫生 英文 可能 說 得 不 好，但是
應該 都 聽得懂。

Zhèlǐ de yīshēng Yīngwén kěnéng shuō de bù hǎo,
dànshì yīnggāi dōu tīngdedǒng.

这里 的 大夫 英文 可能 说 得 不 好，但是
应该 都 听得懂。

The doctors here may not speak English well, but they
should understand everything they hear.

Explaining Outpatient Services and Appointments ▍ 介紹門診和掛號

 王 醫生 星期一 上午、星期五 下午 和 晚上 都 有 門診。

Wáng yīshēng xīngqíyī shàngwǔ, xīngqíwǔ xiàwǔ hé wǎnshang dōu yǒu ménzhěn.

王 大夫 星期一 上午、星期五 下午 和 晚上 都 有 门诊。

Dr. Wang has outpatient appointments Monday mornings, Friday afternoons and nights.

 你 最好 先 用 電話 或 **網路** 掛號，**免得** 現場 掛 不 到 號。

Nǐ zuìhǎo xiān yòng diànhuà huò wǎnglù guàhào, miǎnde xiànchǎng guà budào hào.

你 最好 先 用 电话 或 网络 挂号，免得 现场 挂 不 到 号。

It would be best if you make an appointment by phone or online first to make sure you'll be able to get in to see doctor.

 如果 醫生 **接受** 掛號，就 會 把 病人 都 看完。

Rúguǒ yīshēng jiēshou guàhào, jiù huì bǎ bìngrén dōu kànwán.

如果 大夫 接受 挂号，就 会 把 病人 都 看完。

This doctor sees all of the patients that register.

Keyword				
網路	wǎnglù	网络	internet	N
免得	miǎnde	免得	so as not to	Conj
接受	jiēshòu	接受	to accept	V

The Location of a Pharmacy, Hospital, or Clinic
▌醫療診所的地點

 轉角 就 有 一 家 藥局。

Zhuánjiǎo jiù yǒu yì jiā yàojú.

转角 就 有 一 家 药局。

There's a pharmacy right around the corner.

 你 可能 要 走到 忠孝 路 才 有 牙科 诊所。

Ní kěnéng yào zǒudào Zhōngxiào lù cái yǒu yákē zhénsuǒ.

你 可能 要 走到 忠孝 路 才 有 牙科 诊所。

You might have to go to Zhongxiao Road to find a dentist's office.

 從 這兒 到 台大 醫院 搭 捷運 只要 十 分鐘。

Cóng zhèr dào Táidà Yīyuàn dā jiéyùn zhǐyào shí fēnzhōng.

从 这儿 到 台大 医院 搭 捷运 只要 十 分钟。

It only takes ten minutes to get to National Taiwan University Hospital from here by MRT (subway).

Keyword				
轉角	zhuǎnjiǎo	转角	corner	N

Answers to Questions about Fees and Payment
▌ 有關費用的回答

 看 你 保 的 是 哪 種 險，但是 應該 包括 在 理賠 項目 裡面。

Kàn ní bǎo de shì ná zhóng xiǎn, dànshì yīnggāi bāokuò zài lǐpéi xiàngmù lǐmian.

看 你 保 的 是 哪 种 险，但是 应该 包括 在 理赔 项目 里面。

It depends on your insurance policy, but your fee should be covered.

 我們 收 信用卡。

Wǒmen shōu xìnyòngkǎ.

我们 收 信用卡。

We accept credit cards.

 我們 不 收 信用卡 和 支票。

Wǒmen bù shōu xìnyòngkǎ hé zhīpiào.

我们 不 收 信用卡 和 支票。

We don't accept credit cards or personal checks.

Keyword				
支票	zhīpiào	支票	check	N

掛號費 是 一百 二十 元，再 加上 藥 錢，
一共 是 八百 元。

Guàhàofèi shì yìbǎi èrshí yuán, zài jiāshang yào qián, yígòng shì bābǎi yuán.

挂号费 是 一百 二十 元，再 加上 药 钱，
一共 是 八百元。

The appointment fee is NT$120. Including the medication, it all comes to NT$800.

 這 張 繳費單 包括 所有 項目。

Zhè zhāng jiǎofèidān bāokuò suóyǒu xiàngmù.

这 张 缴费单 包括 所有 项目。

This bill includes everything.

 如果 沒有 健保，基本 費用 會 貴 一點兒，
而且 不 包括 藥 錢。

Rúguǒ méiyǒu jiànbǎo, jīběn fèiyòng huì guì yìdiǎr, érqiě bù bāokuò yào qián.

如果 没有 健保，基本 费用 会 贵 一点儿，
而且 不 包括 药 钱。

If you don't have health insurance, the basic fee will be a little more, and that doesn't include the cost of medication.

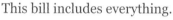

Keyword				
繳費單	jiǎofèidān	缴费单	payment notice	N
基本	jīběn	基本	basic	Vs-attr

Telling where Medicines Are in the Drugstore
▍藥房對藥品位置的回答

 在 第 三 排 **走道** 的 中間。
Zài dì sān pái zǒudào de zhōngjiān.
在 第 三 排 走道 的 中间。
It's in the middle of aisle three.

 你 從 第 一 排 **走道** 過去，就 在 你 的
右手邊。
Nǐ cóng dì yī pái zǒudào guòqu, jiù zài nǐ de
yòushǒubiān.
你 从 第 一 排 走道 过去，就 在 你 的
右手边。
Take the first aisle and it'll be on your right.

 跟 我 來。我 告訴 你 放 在 什麼 地方。
Gēn wǒ lái. Wǒ gàosu nǐ fàng zài shénme dìfang.
跟 我 来。我 告诉 你 放 在 什么 地方。
Follow me. I'll show you where it is.

Keyword				
走道	zǒudào	走道	aisle	N

Answers about Medications at the Drugstore
藥房對藥物的回答

 這 個 藥 不但 可以 止痛 還 可以 **止咳**。

Zhèi ge yào búdàn kéyí zhǐtòng hái kéyí zhǐké.

这 个 药 不但 可以 止痛 还 可以 止咳。

This medicine is a pain reliever and cough suppressant as well.

 我們 有 幾 種 治 鼻炎 的 藥，看 你 是 過敏性 的 還是 感冒 **引起** 的。

Wǒmen yǒu jǐ zhǒng zhì bíyán de yào, kàn nǐ shì guòmǐnxìng de háishì gǎnmào yǐnqǐ de.

我们 有 几 种 治 鼻炎 的 药，看 你 是 过敏性 的 还是 感冒 引起 的。

We have a few different sinus medicines. It depends on whether the problem is caused by allergies or a cold.

 我們 有 **凝膠** 和 **軟膏** 可以 治 嘴破[*]。

Wǒmen yǒu níngjiāo hé ruǎngāo kéyǐ zhì zuǐpò.

我们 有 凝胶 和 软膏 可以 治 嘴破。

We have a gel and an ointment that treat cold sores.

* 「嘴破 zuǐpò」：This refers to the entire mouth, inside and out, and not just to the lips. It may be caused by a virus (cold sores), hitting your mouth, or biting your gums.

Keyword				
止咳	zhǐké	止咳	to relieve a cough	Vi
引起	yǐnqǐ	引起	to cause	V
凝膠	níngjiāo	凝胶	gel	N
軟膏	ruǎngāo	软膏	ointment	N

Unit Nine: Answers To Medical Questions (See Unit Four)
單元九：回答醫療專業問題 (針對單元四)

Answers to Questions about Your Condition
▌回答病情

247 你 的 病 最好 住院。

Nǐ de bìng zuìhǎo zhùyuàn.

你 的 病 最好 住院。

With this problem, it would be best if you were hospitalized.

248 你 有 輕微 的 **腦震盪**，但是 不會 有 事 的。

Ní yǒu qīngwéi de nǎozhèndàng, dànshì bú huì yǒu shì de.

你 有 轻微 的 脑震荡，但是 不 会 有 事 的。

You've suffered a small brain concussion, but you're going to be fine.

249 要 **復元** 至少 需要 四 個 禮拜。

Yào fùyuán zhìshǎo xūyào sì ge lǐbài.

要 复元 至少 需要 四 个 礼拜。

Recovery time would take at least four weeks.

Keyword				
腦震盪	nǎozhèndàng	脑震荡	brain concussion	N
復元	fùyuán	复元	to recover your health	Vi

你 先 吃藥 看看，**目前** 不用 開刀。

Nǐ xiān chīyào kànkan, mùqián búyòng kāidāo.

你 先 吃药 看看，目前 不用 开刀。

First try taking medicine. At present surgery isn't necessary.

 如果 一 個 禮拜 以後 還是 不 舒服，就 再 回來 看診。

Rúguǒ yí ge lǐbài yǐhòu háishì bù shūfu, jiù zài huílai kànzhěn.

如果 一个 礼拜 以后 还是 不 舒服，就 再 回来 看诊。

If you don't feel better in a week, come see me again.

 所有 **含有 花生** 的 食物 都 不要 吃。

Suóyǒu hányǒu huāshēng de shíwù dōu búyào chī.

所有 含有 花生 的 食物 都 不要 吃。

Don't eat any foods containing peanuts.

Keyword				
目前	mùqián	目前	at present	N
含有	hányǒu	含有	to contain	V
花生	huāshēng	花生	peanut	N

Answers to Questions about Medicines
▌回答用藥問題

 每 次 吃 兩 顆，一 天 三 次。
Měi cì chī liǎng kē, yì tiān sān cì.
每 次 吃 两 颗，一 天 三 次。
Take two capsules, three times a day.

 藥 每 餐 飯後 吃，睡前 再 吃 一 次。
Yào měi cān fànhòu chī, shuìqián zài chī yí cì.
药 每 餐 饭后 吃，睡前 再 吃 一 次。
Take the medicine after each meal, and once before you go to bed.

 吃 藥 的 這 段 期間 不要 喝 酒。
Chī yào de zhè duàn qíjiān búyào hē jiǔ.
吃 药 的 这 段 期间 不要 喝 酒。
Don't drink alcohol while taking this medication.

這 種 藥 很 安全。

Zhè zhǒng yào hěn ānquán.

这 种 药 很 安全。

This medicine is very safe.

 這 種 藥 應該 空腹 吃。

Zhè zhǒng yào yīnggāi kōngfù chī.

这 种 药 应该 空腹 吃。

This medication should be taken on an empty stomach.

 要是 你 覺得 好 了，這 個 藥 就 可以 不 吃 了。

Yàoshì nǐ juéde hǎo le, zhèi ge yào jiù kéyǐ bù chī le.

要是 你 觉得 好 了，这 个 药 就 可以 不 吃 了。

You can stop taking this tablet as soon as you feel better.

Keyword				
安全	ānquán	安全	safe	Vs
空腹	kōngfù	空腹	on an empty stomach	N

Answers to Questions about Test Results
▌ 回答檢驗疑問

259 報告 結果 沒 辦法 做出 結論。
Bàogào jiéguǒ méi bànfǎ zuòchū jiélùn.
报告 结果 没 办法 做出 结论。
The results were inconclusive.

260 檢驗 結果 呈現 陽性。
Jiǎnyàn jiéguǒ chéngxiàn yángxìng.
检验 结果 呈现 阳性。
The test came back positive.

261 你 的 尿液 檢驗 顯示 尿酸 指數 很 高。
Nǐ de niàoyì jiǎnyàn xiǎnshì niàosuān zhǐshù hěn gāo.
你 的 尿液 检验 显示 尿酸 指数 很 高。
Your urine test showed a high level of uric acid.

Keyword				
檢驗	jiǎnyàn	检验	test	N
陽性	yángxìng	阳性	positive	N
尿液	niàoyì	尿液	urine	N
尿酸指數	niàosuān zhǐshù	尿酸指数	the exponent of uric acid	◎

Answers to Questions about Surgery
▎回答手術問題

262 手術 是 你 唯一 的 選擇。
Shǒushù shì nǐ wéiyī de xuǎnzé.
手术 是 你 唯一 的 选择。
Surgery is your only option.

263 這 是 個 小 手術，但是 有些 風險。
Zhè shì ge xiáo shǒushù, dànshì yǒuxiē fēngxiǎn.
这 是 个 小 手术，但是 有些 风险。
It's a minor operation, but there are some risks.

264 我們 會 追蹤 你 的 情況，看看 是 不是 非 動手術 不可。
Wǒmen huì zhuīzōng nǐ de qíngkuàng, kànkan shì bushì fēi dòngshǒushù bùkě.
我们 会 追踪 你 的 情况，看看 是 不是 非 动手术 不可。
We will monitor your situation and see if surgery is the way to go.

Keyword				
選擇	xuǎnzé	选择	choice	N
風險	fēngxiǎn	风险	risk	N
追蹤	zhuīzōng	追踪	to follow	V

Answers to Questions about Hospitalization
▌回答住院問題

 一般 探病 時間 是 早上 九 點 到 晚上 九 點。

Yìbān tànbìng shíjiān shì zǎoshang jiú diǎn dào wǎnshang jiú diǎn.

一般 探病 时间 是 早上 九 点 到 晚上 九 点。

Regular visiting hours are from 9 am to 9 pm.

 你 不用 一直 躺 在 床上，你 可以 到 **走廊** 散散步 或 到 外面 坐坐。

Nǐ búyòng yìzhí tǎng zài chuángshang, nǐ kéyǐ dào zǒuláng sànsanbu huò dào wàimian zuòzuo.

你 不用 一直 躺 在 床上，你 可以 到 走廊 散散步 或 到 外面 坐坐。

You don't have to lie on the bed, you can walk in the hallway or sit outdoors.

 醫院 有 **自助 餐廳**、咖啡廳，你 也 可以 吃 家人 準備 的 飯菜。

Yīyuàn yǒu zìzhù cāntīng, kāfēitīng, ní yě kéyǐ chī jiārén zhǔnbèi de fàncài.

医院 有 自助 餐厅、咖啡厅，你 也 可以 吃 家人 准备 的 饭菜。

The hospital has a cafeteria and a coffee shop, or you can eat food your family prepares for you.

Keyword				
走廊	zǒuláng	走廊	hallway	N
自助餐廳	zìzhù cāntīng	自助餐厅	cafeteria	N

Unit Ten: Doctors' Directions
單元十：醫生的指示

Directions at Internal Medicine
▌內科問診時的指示

268 張開 **嘴巴** 說：「啊」。
Zhāngkāi zuǐba shuō: 'ā'.
张开 嘴巴 说：「啊」。
Open your mouth and say "Ahhhh".

269 深呼吸，然後 慢慢 **吐氣**。
Shēnhūxī, ránhòu mànmān tǔqì.
深呼吸，然后 慢慢 吐气。
Take a deep breath and let it out slowly.

270 把 你 的 頭 **轉**到 左邊。
Bá nǐ de tóu zhuǎndào zuǒbian.
把 你 的 头 转到 左边。
Turn your head to the left.

Keyword				
嘴巴	zuǐba	嘴巴	mouth	N
吐氣	tǔqì	吐气	to let out your breath	V-sep
轉	zhuǎn	转	to turn	V

Directions at the Surgery Dept.
外科問診時的指示

 傷口 看起來 很 糟，可能 得 縫 幾 針。

Shāngkǒu kànqǐlai hěn zāo, kěnéng děi féng jǐ zhēn.

伤口 看起来 很 糟，可能 得 缝 几 针。

It looks pretty bad. You might need a few stitches!

 傷口 不要 踫 水，要不然 會 化膿。

Shāngkǒu búyào pèng shuǐ, yàoburán huì huànóng.

伤口 不要 碰 水，要不然 会 化脓。

Don't get the wound wet or it will fester.

 傷口 在 結痂，不要 剝 它。

Shāngkǒu zài jiéjiā, búyào bō tā.

伤口 在 结痂，不要 剥 它。

Don't pick at your scab!

Keyword				
縫	féng	缝	to sew	V
針	zhēn	针	stitch	N
要不然	yàobùrán	要不然	otherwise	Conj
化膿	huànóng	化脓	to fester	Vp
結痂	jiéjiā	结痂	to scab	Vi
剝	bō	剥	to shell	V

Directions about Lifestyle
▌醫生對病人生活習慣的指示

274 多 休息，這 個 禮拜 不要 太 累。
Duō xiūxi, zhèi ge lǐbài búyào tài lèi.
多 休息，这 个 礼拜 不要 太 累。
Rest up. Don't do anything too strenuous this week.

275 多 喝 流質，最好 是 喝 水 和 茶。
Duō hē liúzhí, zuìhǎo shì hē shuǐ hé chá.
多 喝 流质，最好 是 喝 水 和 茶。
Drink plenty of fluids. Water and tea are best.

276 未來 這 幾 天 飲食 要 保持 清淡。
Wèilái zhè jǐ tiān yǐnshí yào bǎochí qīngdàn.
未来 这 几 天 饮食 要 保持 清淡。
Stick to bland food for the next few days.

Keyword				
流質	liúzhí	流质	liquid diet	N
未來	wèilái	未来	future	N
飲食	yǐnshí	饮食	food and beverages	N
清淡	qīngdàn	清淡	light	Vs

Directions about Taking Blood and Injections
▌抽血或注射時的指示

277 手 伸出來，放輕鬆。
Shǒu shēnchūlai, fàngqīngsōng.
手 伸出来，放轻松。
Hold your arm out and try to relax.

278 把 你 的 手 轉過來，握緊 拳頭。
Bá nǐ de shǒu zhuǎnguòlai, wòjǐn quántou.
把 你 的 手 转过来，握紧 拳头。
Turn your arm out and make a fist.

279 用 棉花 按住，手 彎起來。
Yòng miánhuā ànzhù, shǒu wānqǐlai.
用 棉花 按住，手 弯起来。
Hold this cotton ball on your arm and bent it.

Keyword				
伸	shēn	伸	to stretch	V
握緊	wòjǐn	握紧	to grip	V
拳頭	quántou	拳头	fist	N
棉花	miánhuā	棉花	cotton ball	N
按住	ànzhù	按住	to press	V

Directions During Examinations
▌ 檢查時的指示

280 請 穿上 這 件 袍子。
Qǐng chuānshang zhè jiàn páozi.
请 穿上 这 件 袍子。
Please put on this gown.

281 請 躺 在 檢驗台 上。
Qǐng tǎng zài jiǎnyàntái shang.
请 躺 在 检验台 上。
Please lie down on the examination table.

282 會 有 一點兒 不 舒服，但是 不要 動。
Huì yǒu yìdiǎr bù shūfu, dànshì búyào dòng.
会 有 一点儿 不 舒服，但是 不要 动。
This will feel a little bit uncomfortable, but please don't move.

Keyword				
袍子	páozi	袍子	gown	N
檢驗台	jiǎnyàntái	检验台	examination table	N

Diagnoses at Orthopedics ▍ 骨科問診時的判斷

283 看起來 你 的 肩膀 脫臼 了。
Kànqǐlai nǐ de jiānbǎng tuōjiù le.
看起来 你 的 肩膀 脱臼 了。
It looks like you have a dislocated shoulder.

284 你 的 腳 需要 上 八 個 禮拜 的 石膏。
Nǐ de jiǎo xūyào shàng bā ge lǐbài de shígāo.
你 的 脚 需要 上 八 个 礼拜 的 石膏。
Your leg will be in a cast for eight weeks.

285 骨頭 碎 得 很 嚴重，必須 動 手術。
Gútou suì de hěn yánzhòng, bìxū dòng shǒushù.
骨头 碎 得 很 严重，必须 动 手术。
This fracture is really severe. You'll need surgery.

Keyword				
上	shàng	上	to wear (a cast)	V
骨頭	gútou	骨头	bone	N
碎	suì	碎	to break into pieces	Vp
必須	bìxū	必须	must	Vaux

Diagnoses at the Dentistry Dept.
▌牙科問診時的判斷

 你 的 牙 蛀 得 太 厲害，要 拔掉。

Nǐ de yá zhù de tài lìhai, yào bádiào.

你 的 牙 蛀 得 太 厉害，要 拔掉。

Your tooth is too decayed. We'll have to remove it.

 還好 你 來 得 早，只要 補起來 就 行 了。

Háihǎo nǐ lái de zǎo, zhǐyào búqǐlai jiù xíng le.

还好 你 来 得 早，只要 补起来 就 行 了。

Good thing you came in. It needs to be filled.

 你 的 牙齒 發炎 了。得 抽 神經*。

Nǐ de yáchǐ fāyán le. Děi chōu shénjīng.

你 的 牙齿 发炎 了。得 抽 神经。

Your tooth is infected. I'll have to do a root canal.

* 「抽神經 chōu shénjīng」: In cases of severe decay, dentists remove the nerve and keep the physical tooth as the base for a false tooth or cap. Because the tissue is removed from the tooth, the nerves governing pain and blood vessels are removed, but the tooth actually still contains some nerve tissue and blood vessels, so in reality a more accurate term for 「牙齒抽神經 yáchǐ chōu shénjīng」 would be 「牙齒根管治療 yáchǐ gēnguǎn zhìliáo」.

Keyword				
蛀	zhù	蛀	to decay	Vi
拔掉	bádiào	拔掉	to pull out	V
抽神經	chōu shénjīng	抽神经	to do a root canal	◎

Diagnoses at Ophthalmology
▌ 眼科問診時的判斷

289 你 感 染 了 角 膜 炎。
Nǐ gánrǎn le jiǎomòyán.
你 感 染 了 角 膜 炎。
You've got ketatitis.

290 你 的 白 內 障 要 開 刀。
Nǐ de báinèizhàng yào kāidāo.
你 的 白 內 障 要 开 刀。
You'll need surgery to remove the cataract.

291 你 可 能 得 了 夜 盲 症。
Ní kěnéng dé le yèmángzhèng.
你 可 能 得 了 夜 盲 症。
You might have night blindness.

Keyword				
感染	gǎnrǎn	感染	to infect	V
角膜炎	jiǎomòyán	角膜炎	keratitis	N
白內障	báinèizhàng	白內障	cataract	N
夜盲症	yèmángzhèng	夜盲症	night blindness	N

Directions from 119 Operators
| 119 醫護人員的指示

292 試著 讓 他 保持 清醒。
Shìzhe ràng tā bǎochí qīngxǐng.
试著 让 他 保持 清醒。
Try to keep her awake and alert.

293 把 他 的 頭 抬 高，讓 他 舒服 一點兒。
Bǎ tā de tóu tái gāo, ràng tā shūfu yìdiǎr.
把 他 的 头 抬 高，让 他 舒服 一点儿。
Lift up his head and keep him comfortable.

294 在 醫護人員 到達 以前，不要 移動 傷患。
Zài yīhùrényuán dàodá yǐqián, búyào yídòng shānghuàn.
在 医护人员 到达 以前，不要 移动 伤患。
Don't move the victim until the paramedics arrive.

Keyword				
清醒	qīngxǐng	清醒	awake and alert	Vs
抬高	tái gāo	抬高	to lift	Vi
醫護人員	yīhù rényuán	医护人员	paramedic	N
到達	dàodá	到达	to arrive	V
移動	yídòng	移动	to move	V
傷患	shānghuàn	伤患	victim	N

General Diagnoses—You're Better
▌醫生宣佈結果—病康復了

295 你 一點兒 問題 也 沒有。

Nǐ yìdiǎr wèntí yě méiyǒu.

你 一点儿 问题 也 没有。

There's absolutely nothing wrong with you.

296 恭喜 你，你 已經 完全 好 了。

Gōngxí nǐ, ní yǐjīng wánquán hǎo le.

恭喜 你，你 已经 完全 好 了。

Congratulations, you've recovered completely.

297 你 沒 什麼 好 擔心 的。

Nǐ méi shénme hǎo dānxīn de.

你 没 什么 好 担心 的。

You have nothing to worry about.

Keyword				
完全	wánquán	完全	completely	Adv

General Diagnoses—You're Sick
▌ 醫生宣佈結果—生病了

298 恐怕 比 我們 原來 想 的 還要 嚴重。

Kǒngpà bí wǒmen yuánlái xiǎng de háiyào yánzhòng.

恐怕 比 我们 原来 想 的 还要 严重。

I'm afraid that it's more serious than we thought.

299 你 得 了 輕微 的 扁桃腺炎。

Nǐ dé le qīngwéi de biǎntáoxiànyán.

你 得 了 轻微 的 扁桃腺炎。

You've got a mild case of tonsillitis.

300 他 腦 中 的 一 個 血塊 引起 了 中風。

Tā nǎo zhōng de yí ge xiěkuài yǐnqǐ le zhòngfēng.

他 脑 中 的 一 个 血块 引起 了 中风。

A blood clot in his brain caused the stroke.

Keyword				
恐怕	kǒngpà	恐怕	unfortunately	Adv
扁桃腺炎	biǎntáoxiànyán	扁桃腺炎	tonsillitis	N
腦	nǎo	脑	brain	N
血塊	xiěkuài	血块	clot	N
中風	zhòngfēng	中风	stroke	N

Appendices
附　錄

How to Describe Your Pain?
病痛怎麼說？

Even if you're new to the Chinese language, after familiarizing yourself with this short section you'll find that it's not difficult to say where it hurts. You might have noticed that your beginning Chinese textbook isn't filled with the kind of dialogues that you could use right away at the doctor's office. This is because most textbooks introduce vocabulary and grammar at increasing difficulty. Also, there are just too many scenarios in daily life to include a dialogue for each. But actually, seeing a doctor comes down to letting the doctor know how you feel and the type and severity of your discomfort, and answering questions. After that you get your medicine.

Chinese, is systematic; you can get a lot of mileage out of some simple patterns by substituting key vocabulary items. Furthermore, visiting the doctor's office isn't like attending a dinner party. Most of the time you can speak in simple sentences without worrying about etiquette. Below are some simple sentence patterns.

1. 我 不 舒服。

   Wǒ bù shūfu。

   我 不 舒服。

   I don't feel well.

不舒服 is an extremely vague adjective, but quite suitable for getting the conversation going. When you feel generally ill or are in pain all over bu shufu is clear enough. When a specific body part or organ is the problem, just fill in the corresponding noun. (See the index of body parts.) See below:

| 我 | (body part or organ) | 不 舒服。 |

2. 我 的 頭 很 痛。

Wǒ de tóu hěn tòng。

我 的 头 很 痛。

My head hurts.

痛 is less vague than *bù shūfu*, but corresponds to several different expressions in English: to hurt, to be in pain, to ache, etc. Again, you just need to fill in the body part to make a simple, yet clear sentence:

我 的	(body part or organ)	很 痛。

3. 我 的 手 很 癢。/我 的 手 癢癢 的。

Wǒ de shǒu hěn yǎng./Wǒ de shǒu yángyǎng de。

我 的 手 很 痒。/我 的 手 痒痒 的。

My hand itches.

In addition to *tòng*, there are other sensations that can also be expressed in simple sentences: 癢 (yǎng) itchy/itches、紅 (hóng) red、腫 (zhǒng) swollen/puffed up、脹 (zhàng) bloated/swollen、怪 (guài) strange/to have something wrong with、酸 (suān) sour (of the mouth、暈 (yūn) dizzy/lightheaded. Of course all of these adjectives can be reduplicated and followed with *de*.

我 的	(body part or organ)	很 _____。

or

我 的	(body part or organ)	_____ _____ 的。

* The reduplicated adjective + 的 pattern is similar in meaning, but slightly more colloquial.

4. 我 的 頭 痛 得 很 厲害。

Wǒ de tóu tong de hěn lìhai。

我 的 头 痛 得 很 厉害。

I have a really bad headache.

The adjectives (vs) introduced above are all somewhat vague. The doctor may need you to provide a more specific description. There are several common intensifiers in Chinese that allow you to more specifically describe the degree of the sensation:

很 hěn	+ adjective	Neutral
有 一點兒 yǒu yìdiǎr	+ adjective	A little bit _____.
非常 fēicháng	+ adjective	Very/extremely _____.
adjective	+ 得 很 厲害 de hěn lìhai	Extremely _____.
adjective	+ 得 不得了 de bùdeliǎo	incredibly _____.
adjective	+ 得 受不了 de shòubuliǎo	So _____ that I can't stand it.
我 的　　(body part or organ)		adjective with intensifier.

5. 我 從 上 個 禮拜 開始 就 不 舒服 了。
   Wǒ cóng shàng ge lǐbài kāishǐ jiù bù shūfu le。
   我 从 上 个 礼拜 开始 就 不 舒服 了。
   I haven't been feeling well since point in time.

How long have you not been feeling well? Of course the duration of your symptoms is when your doctor makes a diagnosis and recommends a course of treatment.

我	從　since point in time	開始 就 不 舒服 了。

or

我 的 + body part or organ	從　since point in time	開始 就 不 舒服 了。

6. 我 的 手 割傷 了。

   Wǒ de shǒu gēshāng le.

   我 的 手 割伤 了。

   I cut my hand./There's a cut on my hand.

Here are some common external wounds: 割傷 (gēshāng) to get a cut、扭傷 (niǔshāng) to be sprained、燒傷 (shāoshāng) to be burned、燙傷 (tàngshāng) to be scalded、刺傷 (cìshāng) to be stabbed or pierced、撞傷 (zhuàngshāng) to be hit and wounded….. (See the index of common injuries).

我的	(body part or organ)	injuries	了。

7. 我 的 手 被 紙 割傷 了。

   Wǒ de shǒu bèi zhǐ gēshāng le.

   我 的 手 被 纸 割伤 了。

   I got a paper cut.

The doctor can tell a lot about your wound just by looking, but to speed recovery it's still important to provide as much information as possible about how you were injured. In Chinese, you place the cause before the verb, often using the bei passive construction. For example:

被 刀 割傷
bèi dāo gēshāng
to be cut by a knife

被 火 燒傷
bèi huǒ shāoshāng
to be burnt by fire

被 狗 咬傷
bèi gǒu yǎoshāng
to be bitten by a dog

被 貓 抓傷
bèi māo zhuāshāng
to be scratched by a cat

被 熱水 燙傷
bèi rèshuǐ tàngshāng
to be scalded by hot water

被 鉛筆芯 刺傷
bèi qiānbǐxīn cìshāng
to be stabbed by pencil lead

被 車 撞傷
bèi chē zhuàngshāng
to be hit by a car

打 籃球 被 拉傷
dǎ lánqiú bèi lāshāng
to strain a muscle playing basketball

在 樓梯 上 跌了一跤 摔傷 了
zài lóutī shang diéleyìjiāo shuāishāng le
fell on the stairs and injured yourself

| 我的 + body part or organ | 從 | object causing injury | see the index of injuries) | 了。 |

or

| 我 | doing something | 從 | object causing injury | see the index of injuries) | 了。 |

How do You See a Doctor in Taiwan?
怎麼看醫生？

Patients often complain that after registering you have to wait for what seems like forever. Finally, after just a few minutes with the doctor, you pick up your medicine and head home. Here are some tips for being a savvy patient and having an effective trip to the hospital or clinic:

1. **First, before heading to the clinic or hospital, prepare a list of the following:**
   Detailed information about your problem
   Questions for the doctor
   A record of any recent changes in your health
   Any medications or dietary supplements that you are currently taking

   Here are examples of things you can ask the doctor:

   我 的 手 只要 抬高 就 會 痛，這 是 不是 五十肩？
   Wǒ de shǒu zhǐyào táigāo jiù huì tòng, zhè shì bushì wǔshíjiān?
   我 的 手 只要 抬高 就 会 痛，这 是 不是 五十肩？
   It hurts when I try to lift my arm. Is it frozen shoulder (adhesive capsulitis)?

   我 最近 開始 吃 中藥，有 沒有 關係？
   Wǒ zuìjìn kāishǐ chī zhōngyào, yǒu méiyǒu guānxi?
   我 最近 开始 吃 中药，有 没有 关系？
   Does it matter that I recently started taking Chinese medicine?

   我 手上 痣 的 顏色 變 了，是 不是 有 問題？
   Wó shǒushang zhì de yánsè biàn le, shì bushì yǒu wèntí?
   我 手上 痣 的 颜色 变 了，是 不是 有 问题？
   The mole on my hand changed color. Is this okay?

2. **When you need to see a doctor, be mindful of the doctor's time.**

   Pay close attention to main points. Be clear with your descriptions.

   Ask questions, and communicate proactively.

   Take notes about the important things the doctor says.

   Here are some more examples of things you could say:

   我 聽 不 太 懂，請 再 說 一 次。

   Wǒ tīng bú tài dǒng, qǐng zài shuō yí cì.

   我 听 不 太 懂，请 再 说 一 次。

   I don't quite understand. Please say that again.

   我 平常 吃 的 中藥 可以 繼續 吃 嗎？

   Wǒ píngcháng chī de zhōngyào kéyǐ jìxù chī ma?

   我 平常 吃 的 中药 可以 继续 吃 吗?

   Can I keep taking the Chinese medicine that I normally take?

   請 說 慢 一點，我 想 把 它 寫 下來。

   Qǐng shuō màn yìdiǎn, wó xiáng bǎ tā xiě xiàlai.

   请 说 慢 一点，我 想 把 它 写 下来。

   Please speak a little more slowly. I'd like to write this down.

3. **Remember the following points after seeing the doctor**
Keep copies of the medical records and test results that you receive.
Ask for a second opinion.
When you pick up medicine, be sure to listen carefully to the dispensary's explanation.
Take medicine according to the doctor's instructions.
Take note of any side effects of using a medicine and notify the doctor.

You could say the following:

我 把 我 上 次 的 檢驗 報告 帶來 了。
Wó bá wǒ shàng cì de jiǎnyàn bàogào dàilái le.
我 把 我 上 次 的 检验 报告 带来 了。
I brought the results of my last test with me.

台大 醫院 的 醫生 說 這 得 開刀，您 覺得 呢？
Táidà Yīyuàn de yīshēng shuō zhè děi kāidāo, nín juéde ne?
台大 医院 的 医生 说 这 得 开刀，您 觉得 呢？
A doctor at National Taiwan University Hospital said that I need surgery. What do you think?

上 次 開 的 藥 吃 了 以後 會 很 想 睡覺。
Shàng cì kāi de yào chī le yǐhòu huì hén xiǎng shuìjiào.
上 次 开 的 药 吃 了 以後 会 很 想 睡觉。
The medicine you gave me last time made me drowsy.

Human Body Diagrams and Keywords
人體器官圖片與單字片語

Human body
人體

Anterior view 前視

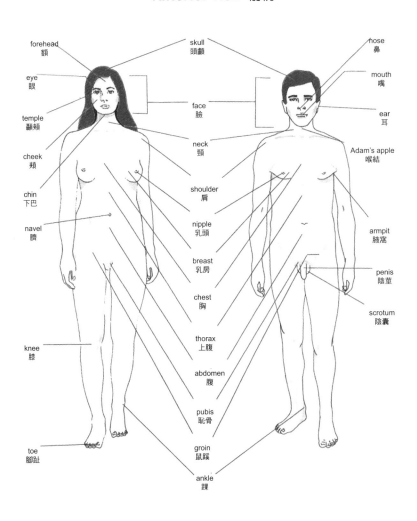

forehead
額

skull
頭顱

nose
鼻

eye
眼

mouth
嘴

temple
顳頰

face
臉

ear
耳

cheek
頰

neck
頸

Adam's apple
喉結

chin
下巴

shoulder
肩

navel
臍

nipple
乳頭

armpit
腋窩

breast
乳房

penis
陰莖

chest
胸

scrotum
陰囊

knee
膝

thorax
上腹

abdomen
腹

toe
腳趾

pubis
恥骨

groin
鼠蹊

ankle
踝

1. Human body 人體—anterior view 前視

1	額	é	额	forehead
2	眼	yǎn	眼	eye
3	顳顬	nièjiá	颞颥	temple
4	頰	jiá	颊	cheek
5	下巴	xiàbā	下巴	chin
6	臍	qí	脐	navel
7	膝	xī	膝	knee
8	腳趾	jiǎozhǐ	脚趾	toe
9	頭顱	tóulú	头颅	skull
10	臉	liǎn	脸	face
11	頸	jǐng	颈	neck
12	肩	jiān	肩	shoulder
13	乳頭	rǔtóu	乳头	nipple
14	乳房	rǔfáng	乳房	breast
15	胸	xiōng	胸	chest
16	上腹	shàngfù	上腹	thorax
17	腹	fù	腹	abdomen
18	恥骨	chǐgǔ	耻骨	pubis
19	鼠蹊	shǔxī	鼠蹊	groin
20	踝	huái	踝	ankle
21	鼻	bí	鼻	nose
22	嘴	zuǐ	嘴	mouth
23	耳	ěr	耳	ear
24	喉結	hóujié	喉结	Adam's apple
25	腋窩	yìwō	腋窝	armpit
26	陰莖	yīnjīng	阴茎	penis
27	陰囊	yīnnáng	阴囊	scrotum

Posterior view 後視

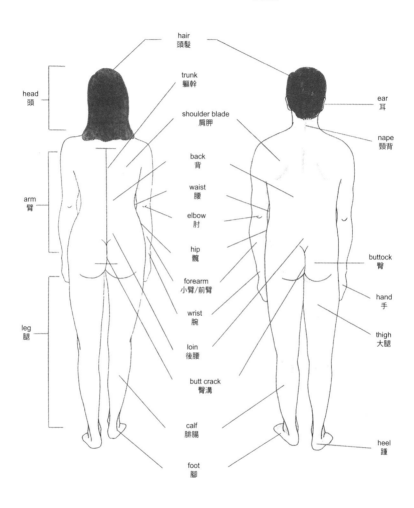

head
頭

hair
頭髮

trunk
軀幹

shoulder blade
肩胛

ear
耳

nape
頸背

arm
臂

back
背

waist
腰

elbow
肘

hip
髖

buttock
臀

leg
腿

forearm
小臂/前臂

wrist
腕

hand
手

loin
後腰

thigh
大腿

butt crack
臀溝

calf
腓腸

heel
踵

foot
腳

2. Human body 人體—posterior view 後視

1	頭	tóu	头	head
2	臂	bèi/bì	臂	arm
3	腿	tuǐ	腿	leg
4	頭髮	tóufǎ	头发	hair
5	軀幹	qūgàn	躯干	trunk
6	肩胛	jiānjiǎ	肩胛	shoulder blade
7	背	bèi	背	back
8	腰	yāo	腰	waist
9	肘	zhǒu	肘	elbow
10	髖	kuān	髋	hip
11	小臂/前臂	xiǎobèi/qiánbèi	小臂/前臂	forearm
12	腕	wàn	腕	wrist
13	後腰	hòuyāo	後腰	loin
14	臀溝	túngōu	臀沟	butt crack
15	腓腸	féicháng	腓肠	calf
16	腳	jiǎo	脚	foot
17	耳	ěr	耳	ear
18	頸背	jǐngbèi	颈背	nape
19	臀	tún	臀	buttock
20	手	shǒu	手	hand
21	大腿	dàtuǐ	大腿	thigh
22	踵	zhǒng	踵	heel

Skeleton 骨骼

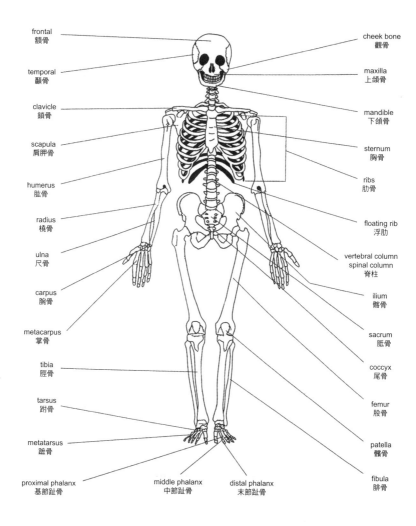

frontal
額骨

temporal
顳骨

clavicle
鎖骨

scapula
肩胛骨

humerus
肱骨

radius
橈骨

ulna
尺骨

carpus
腕骨

metacarpus
掌骨

tibia
脛骨

tarsus
跗骨

metatarsus
蹠骨

proximal phalanx
基節趾骨

middle phalanx
中節趾骨

distal phalanx
末節趾骨

cheek bone
觀骨

maxilla
上頜骨

mandible
下頜骨

sternum
胸骨

ribs
肋骨

floating rib
浮肋

vertebral column
spinal column
脊柱

ilium
髂骨

sacrum
胝骨

coccyx
尾骨

femur
股骨

patella
髕骨

fibula
腓骨

3. Skeleton 骨骼—anterior view 前視

1	額骨	égǔ	额骨	frontal
2	顳骨	nièofǔ	颞骨	temporal
3	鎖骨	suǒgǔ	锁骨	clavicle
4	肩胛骨	jiānjiǎgǔ	肩胛骨	scapula
5	肱骨	gōnggǔ	肱骨	humerus
6	橈骨	ráogǔ	桡骨	radius
7	尺骨	chǐgǔ	尺骨	ulna
8	腕骨	wàngǔ	腕骨	carpus
9	掌骨	zhǎnggǔ	掌骨	metacarpus
10	脛骨	jìnggǔ	胫骨	tibia
11	跗骨	fū gǔ	跗骨	tarsus
12	蹠骨	zhígǔ	跖骨	metatarsus
13	基節趾骨	jījié zhǐgǔ	基节趾骨	proximal phalanx
14	中節趾骨	zhōngjié zhǐgǔ	中节趾骨	middle phalanx
15	末節趾骨	mòjié zhǐgǔ	末节趾骨	distal phalanx
16	顴骨	quángǔ	颧骨	cheek bone
17	上頜骨	shànghàngǔ	上颌骨	maxilla
18	下頜骨	xiàhàngǔ	下颌骨	mandible
19	胸骨	xiōnggǔ	胸骨	sternum
20	肋骨	lègǔ	肋骨	ribs
21	浮肋	fúlè	浮肋	floating rib
22	脊柱	jǐzhù	脊柱	vertebral column spinal column
23	髂骨	kàgǔ	髂骨	ilium
24	骶骨	zhīgǔ	骶骨	sacrum
25	尾骨	wěigǔ	尾骨	coccyx
26	股骨	gǔgǔ	股骨	femur
27	髕骨	bìngǔ	髌骨	patella
28	腓骨	féigǔ	腓骨	fibula

Digestive system 消化系統

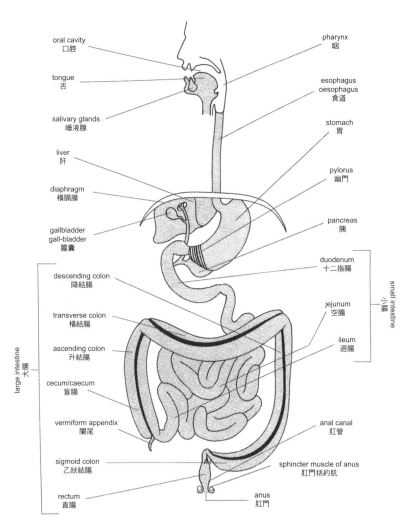

oral cavity
口腔

pharynx
咽

tongue
舌

esophagus
oesophagus
食道

salivary glands
唾液腺

stomach
胃

liver
肝

pylorus
幽門

diaphragm
橫膈膜

pancreas
胰

gallbladder
gall-bladder
膽囊

duodenum
十二指腸

descending colon
降結腸

jejunum
空腸

transverse colon
橫結腸

ileum
迴腸

ascending colon
升結腸

small intestine
小腸

cecum/caecum
盲腸

large intestine
大腸

vermiform appendix
闌尾

anal canal
肛管

sigmoid colon
乙狀結腸

sphincter muscle of anus
肛門括約肌

rectum
直腸

anus
肛門

4. Digestive system 消化系統

1	口腔	kǒuqiāng	口腔	oral cavity
2	舌	shé	舌	tongue
3	唾液腺	tuòyìxiàn	唾液腺	salivary glands
4	肝	gān	肝	liver
5	橫膈膜	hénggémò	橫膈膜	diaphragm
6	膽囊	dǎnnáng	胆囊	gallbladder gall-bladder
7	大腸	dàcháng	大肠	large intestine
8	降結腸	jiàngjiécháng	降结肠	descending colon
9	橫結腸	héngjiécháng	橫结肠	transverse colon
10	升結腸	shēngjiécháng	升结肠	ascending colon
11	盲腸	mángcháng	盲肠	cecum/caecum
12	闌尾	lánwěi	阑尾	(vermiform) appendix
13	乙狀結腸	yǐzhuàng jiécháng	乙状结肠	sigmoid colon
14	直腸	zhícháng	直肠	rectum
15	咽	yān	咽	pharynx
16	食道	shídào	食道	esophagus oesophagus
17	胃	wèi	胃	stomach
18	幽門	yōumén	幽门	pylorus
19	胰	yí	胰	pancreas
20	小腸	xiǎocháng	小肠	small intestine
21	十二指腸	shíèrzhǐcháng	十二指肠	duodenum
22	空腸	kōngcháng	空肠	jejunum
23	迴腸	huícháng	回肠	ileum
24	肛管	gāngguǎn	肛管	anal canal
25	肛門括約肌	gāngmén kuòyuējī	肛门括约肌	sphincter muscle of anus
26	肛門	gāngmén	肛门	anus

Sense organs: hearing
感覺器官：聽覺

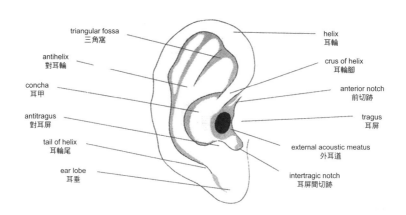

External ear 外耳

1	三角窩	sānjiǎowō	三角窝	triangular fossa
2	對耳輪	duìěrlún	对耳轮	antihelix
3	耳甲	ěrjiǎ	耳甲	concha
4	對耳屏	duìěrpíng	对耳屏	antitragus
5	耳輪尾	ěrlúnwěi	耳轮尾	tail of helix
6	耳垂	ěrchuí	耳垂	ear lobe
7	耳輪尾	ěrlúnwěi	耳轮尾	helix
8	耳輪腳	ěrlúnjiǎo	耳轮脚	crus of helix
9	前切跡	qiánqiējī	前切迹	anterior notch
10	耳屏	ěrpíng	耳屏	tragus
11	外耳道	wàiěrdào	外耳道	external acoustic meatus
12	耳屏間切跡	ěrpíngjiānqiējī	耳屏间切迹	intertragic notch

Sense organs: sight
感覺器官：視覺

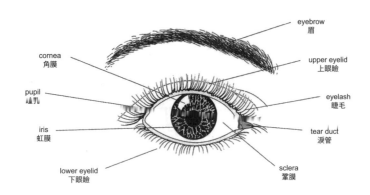

Eyes 眼

1	角膜	jiǎomò	角膜	cornea
2	瞳孔	tóngkǒng	瞳孔	pupil
3	虹膜	hóngmò	虹膜	iris
4	下眼瞼	xiàyǎnjiǎn	下眼睑	lower eyelid
5	眉	méi	眉	eyebrow
6	上眼瞼	shàng yǎnjiǎn	上眼睑	upper eyelid
7	睫毛	jiémáo	睫毛	eyelash
8	淚管	lèiguǎn	泪管	tear duct
9	鞏膜	gǒngmò	巩膜	sclera

Sense organs: taste
感覺器官：味覺

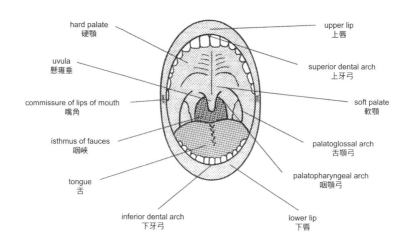

hard palate 硬顎		upper lip 上唇
uvula 懸雍垂		superior dental arch 上牙弓
commissure of lips of mouth 嘴角		soft palate 軟顎
isthmus of fauces 咽峽		palatoglossal arch 舌顎弓
tongue 舌		palatopharyngeal arch 咽顎弓
inferior dental arch 下牙弓		lower lip 下唇

Mouth 口

1	硬顎	yìng'è	硬颚	hard palate
2	懸雍垂	xuányōngchuí	悬雍垂	uvula
3	嘴角	zǔijiǎo	嘴角	commissure of lips of mouth
4	咽峽	yānxiá	咽峡	isthmus of fauces
5	舌	shé	舌	tongue
6	下牙弓	xiàyágōng	下牙弓	inferior dental arch
7	上唇	shàngchún	上唇	upper lip
8	上牙弓	shàngyágōng	上牙弓	superior dental arch
9	軟顎	ruǎn'è	软颚	soft palate
10	舌顎弓	shéègōng	舌颚弓	palatoglossal arch
11	咽顎弓	yān'ègōng	咽颚弓	palatopharyngeal arch
12	下唇	xiàchún	下唇	lower lip

Sense organs: smell
感覺器官：嗅覺

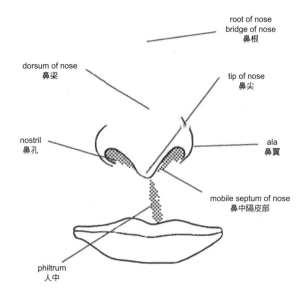

root of nose
bridge of nose
鼻根

dorsum of nose
鼻梁

tip of nose
鼻尖

nostril
鼻孔

ala
鼻翼

mobile septum of nose
鼻中隔皮部

philtrum
人中

External nose 外鼻

1	鼻梁	bíliáng	鼻梁	dorsum of nose
2	鼻孔	bíkǒng	鼻孔	nostril
3	人中	rénzhōng	人中	philtrum
4	鼻根	bígēn	鼻根	root of nose bridge of nose
5	鼻尖	bíjiān	鼻尖	tip of nose
6	鼻翼	bíyì	鼻翼	ala
7	鼻中隔皮部	bízhōnggépíbù	鼻中隔皮部	mobile septum of nose

Medical Treatment:Vocabulary & Phrases
醫療相關單字片語

Commonly used household medicines
居家常用藥

消炎藥膏	xiāoyán yàogāo	消炎药膏	antiseptic cream
優碘	yōudiǎn	优碘	aqua beta-iodine
繃帶	bēngdài	绷带	bandage
OK繃	OKbēng	OK绷	Band-aids
雙氧水	shuāngyǎngshuǐ	双氧水	hydrogen peroxide
藥用酒精	yàoyòng jiǔjīng	药用酒精	medicinal alcohol
紅藥水	hóngyàoshuǐ	红药水	mercurochrome
生理食鹽水	shēnglǐ shíyánshuǐ	生理食盐水	physiological saline
貼布	tiēbù	贴布	plaster
消毒脫脂棉花	xiāodú tuōzhī mianhuā	消毒脱脂棉花	sterilized absorbent cotton
消毒脫脂紗布	xiāodú tuōzhī shābú	消毒脱脂纱布	sterilized absorbent gauze
抗生素	kàngshēngsú	抗生素	antibiotic
止瀉藥	zhǐxièyào	止泻药	anti-diarrhoea
阿斯匹靈	āsīpīlíng	阿斯匹灵	asprin
過敏藥	guòmǐnyào	过敏药	calamin
咳嗽藥水	késòuyàoshuǐ	咳嗽药水	cough syrup
消化藥	xiāohuàyào	消化药	digestant
眼藥水	yǎnyàoshuǐ	眼药水	eye drops
療黴舒乳膏（香港腳藥膏）	liáoméishūrǔgāo (xiānggǎngjiǎo yàogāo)	疗霉舒乳膏（香港脚药膏）	Lamisil cream

| 暈車藥 | yūnchēyào | 晕车药 | motion sickness medicine |
| 普拿疼 | pǔnáténg | 普拿疼 | panadol |

Common symptoms
常見症狀

頭痛欲裂	tóutòng yùliè	头痛欲裂	to have a splitting headache
頭暈目眩	tóuyūn mùxuan	头晕目眩	to feel dizzy
刺痛	cìtòng	刺痛	to feel a sharp piercing pain
頭暈	tóuyūn	头晕	to feel light-headed/dizzy
鼻塞	bísāi	鼻塞	to have a stuffy nose
流鼻血	liú bíxiě	流鼻血	to get a nosebleed
流鼻水	liú bíshuǐ	流鼻水	to have a runny nose
耳鳴	ěrmíng	耳鸣	to have a ringing in your ears
喉嚨癢	hóulóng yǎng	喉咙痒	to have a scratchy throat
過敏	guòmǐn	过敏	to be allergic
癢	yǎng	痒	to itch
起疹子	qǐ zhěnzi	起疹子	to get a rash
背痛	bèitòng	背痛	to have a backache (upper back)
腰痛	yāotòng	腰痛	to have a backache (lower back)
脹氣	zhàngqì	胀气	to be bloated
肚子陣痛	dùzi zhèntòng	肚子阵痛	to have bouts of abdominal pain
拉肚子	lā dùzi	拉肚子	to have diarrhea

便秘	biànmì	便秘	to be constipated
刺傷	cìshāng	刺伤	to get a wound from stabbing
瘀傷	yūshāng	瘀伤	to get a bruise
燙傷/燒傷/曬傷	tàngshāng/ shāoshāng/ shàishāng	烫伤/烧伤/晒伤	to be scalded/ to be burned (by fire)/ to get a sunburn
噎住	yēzhù	噎住	to choke
口臭	kǒuchòu	口臭	to have a foul taste in your mouth
嘴角破	zuǐjiǎo pò	嘴角破	to have cracks at the corners of mouth/ to have cold sores
咳嗽	késòu	咳嗽	to cough
咳嗽帶痰	késòu dài tán	咳嗽带痰	to cough up phlegm
昏倒	hūndǎo	昏倒	to faint
想吐	xiǎngtù	想吐	to feel nauseous
做惡夢	zuò èmèng	做恶梦	to have nightmares
發燒	fāshāo	发烧	to have a fever
發冷	fālěng	发冷	to have chills
頭痛	tóutòng	头痛	to have a headache
喉嚨痛	hóulóng tòng	喉咙痛	to have a sore throat
聲音沙啞	shēngyīn shāyǎ	声音沙哑	to be hoarse
沒有力氣	méiyǒu lìqì	没有力气	to feel weak
發炎	fāyán	发炎	to be inflamed/irritated
沒有食慾	méiyǒu shíyù	没有食欲	don't have an appetite
噁心	ěxīn	噁心	to feel nauseous
盜汗	dàohàn	盗汗	to have night sweats

吞嚥困難	tūnyàn kùnnán	吞咽困难	to have trouble swallowing
脫皮	tuōpí	脱皮	your skin is peeling
燙傷	tàngshāng	烫伤	to be scalded
擦傷	cāshāng	擦伤	to get a scrape
休克	xiūkè	休克	to be in shock
呼吸急促	hūxī jícù	呼吸急促	to be short of breath
扭傷	niǔshāng	扭伤	to get a sprain/twisted joint
肩膀僵硬	jiānbǎng jiāngyìng	肩膀僵硬	to have a stiff shoulder
胸悶	xiōngmēn	胸闷	to feel tightness in the chest
出冷汗	chū lěnghàn	出冷汗	to break out in a cold sweat
放屁	fàngpì	放屁	to fart
打嗝	dǎgé	打嗝	to hiccup
打噴嚏	dǎpēntì	打喷嚏	to sneeze
出汗	chūhàn	出汗	to sweat
牙痛	yátòng	牙痛	to have a toothache
失去知覺	shīqù zhījué	失去知觉	to go unconscious
視線模糊	shìxiàn móhú	视线模糊	to have blurry vision
疲倦	píjuàn	疲倦	to feel fatigued
體重減輕	tǐzhòng jiǎnqīng	体重减轻	to lose weight
頭昏眼花	tóuhūn yǎnhuā	头昏眼花	to be dizzy and have unclear vision

Situational Chinese: Phone Calls and Letters

This book includes 600 examples for your immediate use based on common everyday situations— making an appointment, leaving a voicemail message, filing a complaint, congratulations, consolation letter, etc.

ISBN 978-957-445-360-3
US$ 13.00

Situational Chinese: Traveling

This book starts from simple sentences, gradually adding complexity to help you learn very useful Chinese sentences which will allow you to immediately utilize and grasp new phrases and vocabulary for traveling purposes.

ISBN 978-957-445-362-7
US$ 10.00

ISBN 978-957-445-361-0
US$ 13.00

Situational Chinese: Shopping & Eating Out

The primary objective of this book is to equip you with a unique set of Chinese skills that can be used in a wide variety of shopping and bargaining situations.
The Eating Out section covers fundamental topics including basic expressions of hunger, how to accept and reject invitations, order a meal, cope with different dining environments, make a toast, and handle the bill.

ISBN 978-957-445-391-7
US$ 13.00

Situational Chinese: Workplace

The purpose of this book is to help you, in the shortest time possible, to master 600 important sentence patterns which can be used in workplace situations.

ISBN 978-957-445-392-4
US$ 13.00

Situational Chinese: Business and Business Travel

This is a quick-reference tool containing many of the most relevant and commonly used Chinese phrases for traveling to Chinese-speaking countries on business. We have taken great care to create this convenient quick-reference tool and hope it will come in handy when you pass through customs, exchange money, meet business contacts, place product orders, or attend your first 尾牙 (year-end "Tail Tooth" party)!

ISBN 978-957-445-393-1
US$ 13.00

Situational Chinese: Campus Life and Socializing

This book is intended to help students newly arrived in Taiwan to acquire, as quickly as possible, the basic conversational skills they will need to start forming new friendships. It is through conversational skills that the fascinating world of friendship and culture will truly begin to open.

ISBN 978-957-445-394-8
US$ 10.00

Situational Chinese: Medical Treatment

No matter what your current level of Chinese is, this practical little book will prove an indispensable companion for life in Chinese-speaking placcs. It provides concise phrases and sentences that you may find immediately useful. It is organized into sections that correspond to different medical needs which makes it useful in any common medical situation.